John Alexander Steuart

Letters to Living Authors

John Alexander Steuart

Letters to Living Authors

ISBN/EAN: 9783744688451

Printed in Europe, USA, Canada, Australia, Japan

Cover: Foto ©Thomas Meinert / pixelio.de

More available books at **www.hansebooks.com**

LETTERS

TO

LIVING AUTHORS

BY

JOHN A. STEUART

AUTHOR OF 'SELF-EXILED,' ETC.

WITH PORTRAITS

LONDON

SAMPSON LOW, MARSTON, SEARLE, & RIVINGTON

Limited

St. Dunstan's House

FETTER LANE, FLEET STREET, E.C.

1890

TO

E. HOWARD

THIS VOLUME IS INSCRIBED

CONTENTS

The Publishers beg to acknowledge their indebtedness to Messrs. ELLIOTT & FRY *for permission to copy many of their Portraits of Authors given in this Volume.*

LETTERS
TO LIVING AUTHORS.

To Mr. GEORGE MEREDITH.

Sir,—There is a certain quality which, more than talent, or genius, or energy, or force of will, lies at the bottom of all material success— the quality which is known among men as worldly wisdom. You can scarcely be congratulated on possessing it, for throughout your career you have shown less concern for the comfort and convenience of your patrons, the public, than any other literary caterer living to-day. Indeed, with the exception of Carlyle, no British writer of this generation has been so utterly regardless of the ease of the critics and the pleasure of the general reader You seem perfectly oblivious of the fact that novels, whether written for recreation or not, are, as a rule, most assuredly read for recreation ; and that a work of fiction which does not primarily please, apart from its literary merits, stands but a meagre chance of being read at all. The business of life is not popularly supposed to lie in solving enigmas and puzzling the brain over paradoxes. The British nation is chary—very chary—of making exorbitant demands on its head, especially in matters designed for its entertainment. It has a natural aptitude for enjoyment, and likes to have things made easy for it. Would you be admonished, and gain the popular vote ? Then trouble the reader less with profound intellectual problems ; do not so strenuously insist on his fathoming the great deeps of philosophy ; let the world wag, since it is so careless of its destiny ; in a word, assume the jaunty indifference to all things serious which is so pleasing a characteristic of Mayfair, and study the tastes rather than the needs of mankind.

Most writers, I believe, start with high moral and æsthetic aims. They will regenerate the

graceless sons of Adam ; they will wipe away
the grime of thousands of years of wickedness,
and establish the love of the noble and the
beautiful.   But they speedily discover that the
ungrateful, sons of Adam have really no desire
to be regenerated ; they are content to continue
sinful, and read sensational books full of wild
adventure and intrigue and gore and all the
other reprehensible things that are of so sweet
a savour to the depraved and vulgar palate.
And so the majority of our authors, having an
eye to results, prescribe and supply, not so much
what is needed, as what is demanded.

You are an exception.   You have been
quixotical enough to remain steadfastly true to
your early ideals.   You have given the world,
not what it wanted, but what you thought was
good for it.   You have put intellect into every
sentence you have written, reckless of consequences, therein departing very far indeed from
the glorious traditions of English fiction.   To
say the truth, I think you have been too lofty
in your contempt of the rights and prerogatives
of that well-meaning and not ill-deserving, if
not very intelligent, individual, the habitual

novel reader. Other novelists may occasionally take the bit between their teeth, as it were, and indulge in a gallop .to please themselves, but they quickly slacken down to the conventional ambling pace, and make everything comfortable for the party in the saddle. To change the metaphor, they mostly dilute their draught of thought to suit the taste of consumers ; but you stubbornly persist in for ever giving yours over-proof, perfectly indifferent if people turn away gasping. That is not the way to be popular, and indeed you are at opposite poles from one's ideal of a popular writer.

Your only commodity is thought, which is not in any great demand in the present era. You made a mistake at the beginning, and, less discriminating than many who are your inferiors, you have never seen it. All along you have gone on the assumption that the world is craving for more light, whereas it is rather obscuration and forgetfulness it is seeking. You fancied that on certain weighty and perplexing pro-blems, which lay very near your heart, mankind was pining for enlightenment, and, with the noble audacity of a generous and gifted soul, you undertook to make things clear ; and you have succeeded but too well. That is, you have led the reading public to understand that you are a moral and social reformer, and not a story-teller. But for the ample proof to the contrary contained in your works, your policy might lead one to think that you know little or nothing of human nature. Your course, in a worldly sense, has been the height of inexpediency. You have forgotten, or ignored, or were never aware of a fact well known to, and generally sedulously kept in mind by, every one whose fortune hangs on the public taste,—that the world, even in its direst straits, can hardly be induced to take medicine, except in the form of confections. You might very well have begun by putting your drugs in sweetmeats. In other words, you might have made your *début* with bland and easy commonplace. We pride ourselves upon being a practical and commonplace people,—who hold transcendentalism in contempt ; and depend upon it the man who ministers to our taste will not be without his reward. And you might have had your reward if, instead of following your own inclination, you had bent a little more to ours. But you persevered in your headstrong course, and the result has been precisely what might have been anticipated—you frightened those whom you sought to benefit—so that by the great mass of readers you are still regarded with terror. Very condign punishment indeed overtook you for your rashness; for hardly during the present century has any writer of your intellectual force and fine imaginative power been so long and cruelly neglected. When writers, without a twentieth part of your gifts or your culture, have been shooting aloft into fortune, and what is temporarily taken for fame, you have remained toiling in comparative obscurity, no doubt eagerly panting for appreciation, yet determined to bate not one jot of your independence, or in the smallest particular prove a traitor to your ideal. Happily there are signs that the long-delayed victory is coming at last, that you are gaining recognition, or, to use a cant phrase of criticism, that you 'are swimming into the ken of culture.'

Mr. Besant, in speaking of the hardships of

poor Richard Jefferies, says that it must ultimately be destructive of the highest genius to toil year after year without reward or recognition. He is of opinion that in order to do his best an author must be praised. I don't think it would be hard to show that Mr. Besant is mistaken. At any rate there are a great many exceptions to the rule he would establish. Without going far afield, we have Wordsworth and Carlyle and yourself toiling for many years neglected, or noticed only to be derided, and yet producing works of supreme excellence. When Wordsworth wrote his *Ode to Immortality*, he was not earning enough by his literary labours to buy salt for his porridge (it goes as a matter of course that such a lover of simplicity took porridge); when Carlyle produced his *French Revolution*, it was with some dubitation that the publishers accepted the manuscript; and *The Ordeal of Richard Feverel* was written long before your name had any potency in the republic of letters. It is hard, however, to bear neglect, and you must have had a fine faith in your own intellectual endowments, and the ultimate appreciation of mankind, to have continued the battle so long. But fortunately for the name of England you have now a large number of admirers, a number which is every day increasing, and which no doubt will go on increasing till you take your right place in the literature of your country.

It is a significant fact that while you are admired, and even worshipped, you have not, so far as I know, been imitated. Certain peculiarities of your style are, indeed, creeping into some of our latter-day novels; but your modes of thought, your manner of treatment, your brilliancy of expression, all that is essentially and particularly George Meredith, has been left most severely alone, and for very obvious reasons. Not to speak of the difficulty of copying you (which would be considerable), your style in general is not one to be imitated by the tyro aiming at popularity. 'Some styles,' says Professor Teufelsdröckh, 'are lean, adust, wiry, the muscle itself seems osseous; some are even quite pallid, hunger-bitten, and dead-looking; while others glow in the flush of health and vigorous self-growth, sometimes (as in my own case) not without an apoplectic tendency.'

Yours may be called the apoplectic style, for it is never for one moment to be depended upon. It is jerky, irruptive, full of inequalities. The reader never knows whether he is to be led across flowery meads, or by winding paths through bosky groves, or hurled over a precipice. At times—particularly at the beginning of a book —the manner is so stiff, so rugged, so difficult, that only one who knows what is ahead would persevere. Take for instance the opening of *The Egoist.* It is brilliant, keenly intellectual, full of fine thought and sharp-cut phrases, of wit, of humour, of satire, of every quality, in fact, that ought to make it popular, and yet it is far from being easy reading. It has nothing of the ease that lures, the softness that enchants, the grace that captivates. It were an interesting problem to solve how one who is always so brilliant can be occasionally so repellent. The beginning of *The Egoist* is as discouraging as the beginning of *Sartor Resartus*, and indeed reminds one of that now much lauded, though still little read, book. The dissertation on the Comic Muse is admirable and terrible. An ordinary reader would never wade through that superb first chapter, nor would he (or is it she ?) be able to understand it if he were to read it a score of times. There, and elsewhere throughout your books, one is haunted by the suspicion that you have mistaken your vocation, that you should have taken to some other department of literature ; to history or philosophy or criticism, to anything but story-telling. And you are too fond of making the reader pant after you till he is out of breath if not out of temper. What is an ordinary mortal to make of a sentence like the following ?—

'As when the foreman of a sentimental jury is commissioned to inform an awful bench, exact in perspicuous English, of a verdict that must of necessity be produced in favour of the hanging of the culprit, yet would fain attenuate the crime of a palpable villain by a recommendation to mercy, such foreman, standing in the attentive eye of a master of grammatical construction, and feeling the weight of at least three sentences on his brain, together with a prospect of judicial interrogation for the discovery of his precise meaning, is oppressed, himself is put on trial in turn, and he hesitates, he recapitulates, the fear of involution leads him to be involved ; as far as a man so posted may, he on his own behalf appeals for mercy, entreats that his indistinct statement of preposterous reasons may be taken for understood, and would gladly, were permission to do it credible, throw in an imploring word that he may sink back among the crowd, without for one imperishable moment publicly swinging in his lordship's estimation :—much so, moved by chivalry for a lady, courtesy to the recollection of a hostess, and particularly by the knowledge that his hearer would expect with a certain frigid rigour charity of him, Dr. Middleton paused, spoke and paused, he stammered.'

And the reader is likely to do the same, and to use strong language when he recovers his breath and his self-possession. Would you find a sentence like that in the work of any popular pet, supposing our popular pets capable of writing it? Hardly. It is as bad as Carlyle in his most contemptuous mood, when his aim is to irritate and confuse.

But while you are guilty of these indiscretions, it must be admitted that you have always one great excellence.   As a phrase-maker you have scarcely any living **equal,** certainly no living **superior.**   You can illuminate **a** character or a **scene** in a sentence, and many excellent **proverbs** might be culled from **your writings.**

'She is clever,' says Clara Middleton of Mrs. Mountstuart Jenkinson ; 'she could tattoo me **with epigrams.'**   Which is true.   You shower your epigrams about as if **they** came to you as easily as the dewdrops to the grass.   Pope himself does not **coruscate** more continuously or brilliantly.

'You are cold, my **love** ; you shivered,' says the **Egoïst.**

'I am **not** cold,' answers the wretched **Clara.** 'Some one, I suppose, was walking **over my grave.'**

As suggestive a sentence, I think, as there is in all fiction.   Then one scarcely knows whether most to admire your wit **or** your wisdom.

'A pigmy's a giant if he can manage to **arrive in** season,' is, one would say, a sentence **that is** destined to live.

'No one?' she said, 'am I alone in the house?'

'There is a figure naught,' said he, 'but it's as

good as annihilated, and no figure at all, if you put yourself on the wrong side of it.' A very pretty piece of wit, as Mr. Stevenson would say.

Again : ' He was the very sea-wind for bracing unstrung nerves ' gives as succinct a description of a strong-minded individual as one could well have ; while Mrs. Berry's saying that ' it 's al'ays the plan in a dielemmer to pray God and walk forward ' is as sound a bit of moral philosophy as ever came out of a pulpit. But your good things are not to be picked out like plums from a pudding. They lie so thick that any attempt to extract them must prove futile.

Your success as a wit and phrase-maker, however, exposes you to a danger which you have yourself well described through one of your characters. ' You see how easy it is to deceive one who is an artist in phrases. Avoid them, Miss Dale, they puzzle the penetration of the composer. That is why people of ability like Mrs. Mountstuart Jenkinson ' (and Mr. George Meredith) ' see so little ; they are so bent on describing brilliantly.'

Excessive brilliance is rather an unusual complaint, but it is one from which you frequently suffer. You are too witty to be entirely true to nature, for nature is rather economical in that respect ; and so, though not precisely for the same reason, are most novelists. But with you every boor is a wit, every rustic maid a potential Mrs. Mountstuart Jenkinson. It is delightfully stimulating to the reader, but it is not human nature, a fact which no one knows better than the sinner himself.

This leads to a consideration of how you fulfil the prime function of the novelist—in other words, how you draw character in general. After all, it matters little how magnificent the achievements of a dramatist or novelist be in other respects, if he fail in characterisation he may justly be said to fail in all, because he fails in the first essential of his art. It is the crowning distinction of Shakespeare that he is the best of all portrait-painters ; that every sentence, every word uttered by his characters makes the self-revelation the clearer. And, indeed, the same is true, in a lesser degree, of all the great masters of humanity, of Cervantes, of Scott, of Goethe, of Fielding, of Balzac, of Hawthorne, and the whole illustrious band who discover to us the secrets of the soul. Now you draw character as you do most other things— well; but you are not so eminently, or rather pre-eminently, successful in that line as in some others. The cause, as you will forgive me for saying, is, of course, primarily limitation of faculty. You remember Addison's (or was it Dick Steele's) illustration of the midwife. A writer cannot give what he hasn't got, and he shouldn't be censured for not giving it. But in your case the reason is not wholly limitation of faculty. I have already said that you suffer from excessive brilliancy, and I repeat it with emphasis, with tremenjous emphasis, as Arte-mus Ward would say. Your merit is your defect. Your wit is, in all seriousness, often your bane. In the dazzle of your own bright-ness you are blinded to the qualities of ordi-nary human nature. Clever people you can delineate with anybody, dead or living; but clever people are the few in this world, and dolts are the **many; and** in consequence of your scorn or ignorance of the latter, instead of drawing broad human nature, as Scott does, for example, you draw glittering bits here and there, very beautiful, very attractive, stimulating, altogether delightful in themselves, but giving little more conception of humanity at large than a shooting-star gives of the mysteries of the Solar System, or a piece of sparkling mineral of the wonders of geology. You draw English peasants, for instance, and it is only necessary to compare them to Thomas Hardy's to gauge your success. Mr. Hardy gives us the real true blue—the identical chaw-bacon—who is the backbone of our beloved England; you give the noble animal after he has undergone a clarifying process, and, as the Scottish people say, 'learned some wut.' On the other hand, there are certain strong types of character which you draw with a power which is perhaps unmatched among contemporary English novelists. Sir Willoughby Patterne is one of the most magnificent studies in the whole range of literature. No one who has not read the *Egoist* can fully understand the meaning of selfishness and conceit. But for myself, much as I admire the splendours of the *Egoist*, highly as I delight in *Diana of the Crossways*, and *Rhoda Fleming*, I prefer *Richard Feverel*.

I should be inclined, indeed, to say it is your high-water mark in fiction. It has more humour than is common with you, and also more tenderness. Clare's Diary and the death of Lucy are very affecting, perhaps because of the admirable reticence. How Dickens would have squeezed the sponge in those scenes! Then for humour there is the scamp Adrian, and the escapades of the boys Richard and Ripton.' I think you could have written a good boy's book. (I don't mean a book for good boys.) And for general strength there is Sir Austin, fit to stand beside Sir Willoughby— a great, strong, blind character, blind even to the last, and in the midst of that frightful tragedy which was the logical outcome of his 'System.' I would have that book placed in the hand of every father in the land with a son whose welfare—moral, mental, and material— is dear to him; and I would have readers in general (and moral reformers in particular) put through a course of Mr. George Meredith.

To Dr. OLIVER WENDELL HOLMES.

SIR,—Mr. Swinburne says somewhere that the most beloved of all English writers may be Goldsmith or may be Scott, but the best beloved will always be Charles Lamb. It may be that among American men of letters you are not the most beloved, but I venture to say that there are few, if any, better beloved. Since you rode into fame in that ' Wonderful One-hoss Shay,' with all the world laughing and huzzaing at your heels, you have kept the affections of the peoples of two hemispheres, without lapse and without diminution. Few authors have ever, in their own lifetime, enjoyed so long a lease of unbroken popularity. There have been writers who have risen higher than you in the popular esteem, but most of them were only a kind of literary rockets, that have burned for a moment in the eyes of all men, then fallen and gone out

OLIVER WENDELL HOLMES.

with a hiss and a sputter, leaving one to wonder
at the laws which govern such erratic and altogether inexplicable creations. It were a curious
and interesting and instructive study to trace
the waxing and waning reputations of the past
half-century, to count the number of pseudo-
geniuses who have gone up at the tail of a
newspaper kite, to borrow a happy phrase from
Mr. Lowell, and come down headlong with the
velocity of the first arch-sinner to demonstrate
how very perilous those aerial flights are to them
who have nothing in the shape of natural wings
should anything go wrong with the kite. Since
the beginning of your career as an author many
meteors, to use a somewhat worn but apt and
expressive metaphor, have shot out of darkness,
flashed brilliantly against the sky, and, ere the
critics could adjust their glasses to determine
what the dazzling phenomena might be, have
gone out, leaving only darkness again, and
perhaps a suggestion of sulphur or gunpowder.
Much of this you have seen on all hands. You
have beheld the promising one, the new poet
or the new novelist, soar higher and higher, till
the eye was, perhaps, pained and the head dizzy

watching him, or her; and then all at once you might perceive a tremulous motion, a flutter of the plumage, as it were, a sign of waning force, as if the gas in the balloon were exhausted, and then, suddenly, the inevitable straight-down descent. And while this upward and downward rush has been going on, to the general confusion of mankind, you have held along the pleasant leafy ways of goodly prosperity, never anxious to rise into unnatural altitudes, but always careful to keep out of the ditches, comparatively careless of the company of the gods, but ever on good terms with well-dressed, well-to-do, well-mannered men and women. You move along like a prosperous, good-humoured man of the world, cracking a joke here and there, letting fall, at the proper intervals, delightful morsels of wisdom, so made up and disguised that they shall be taken as confections; not sweet enough, however, to nauseate, nor heavy enough to cause an attack of dyspepsia. You are not commonplace, and you are not eccentric. You have as little of the doleful gravity of the platitudinarian as of the theatrical spirit of the mountebank or the juggler (all of whom flourish in literature in this singular era) : your zeal or your vanity is not so great that you carry anything to excess. You believe in—and, what is more, practise— the golden mean in all things. And this is one cause of your long-continued popularity.

Another cause is that you are one of the most companionable writers in the world—that is, one of the most genial. The sour may say what they like, but the world, as a whole, is in- clined to be agreeable, if only treated cour- teously and fairly. You have the happy knack of pleasing, and on almost all subjects. It is a knack which is not always an attribute of genius. There have been great men who were not plea- sant men. Many well-intentioned folks spoil a truth by their manner of enforcing it. Their truculency raises a spirit of opposition. There is so much of the schoolmaster in their mien that one is for ever expecting to see the birch- rod, and the anxiety to protect the knuckles diverts one's mind from the lesson. The olive- branch may be in front, but one always suspects that there is a sharp switch, or, perhaps, even a cudgel, behind. Truth and morality have little chance under such circumstances. Then there are many teachers and moral philosophers who, while not absolutely truculent, are disconcertingly austere. Mr. Lowell neatly observes in one of his essays that Milton was not a man to be slapped on the back. No, the great Puritan poet, whatever his other qualities may have been, was not remarkable for his sociability. And, since his day, other moral dignitaries and grandees, whose virtues we are all ready to admit, and even to extol when we are not asked nor expected to emulate them, have been so dreadfully severe, so exacting, so illiberal in allowing for the inherited frailties of common humanity, that — well, that we would rather shun their presence if possible. Their ethical codes may be excellent, but their manner is chilly, as if they had passed their youth on icebergs, and had been incurably affected with cold.

With you, who are likewise a teacher, it is wholly different. Warmth and brotherly feeling pervade all you say. You have not that superior consciousness of self-immaculateness which overawes and frightens the humble inquirer in reading the writings of so many estimable authors.

You convey your morals jocosely, and as it were inadvertently, so that the patient swallows the medicine almost without being aware of it. This dexterity, or this geniality, or both combined, have made people look on you as a humorist pure and simple. Mr. George Augustus Sala calls you 'a funny fellow, a very funny fellow.' I own the description does not much please me. It is true, to be sure, as far as it goes, but it does not go far enough. It is apt to give the impression that you aim only at being 'funny,' like Mr. William Nye, whose jokes remind one of the Scotsman's, inasmuch as they are delivered with 'great defeeculty'; or like Mark Twain, in whose work, too, the labour is often much more apparent than the humour. 'Nothing can be more galling to a man's self-respect than to be considered a mere jester,' says a famous countryman of yours. Nothing surely, and you long since saw this. 'If the sense of the ridiculous,' you say in one place, 'is one side of an impressible nature, it is very well; but if that is all there is in a man, he had better have been an ape at once, and so have stood at the head of his profession.   Laughter and tears are meant to turn the wheels of the same machinery of sensibility; one is wind-power, and the other water-power, that is all. . . . Do you know that you feel a little superior to every man who makes you laugh, whether by making faces or verses?   Are you aware that you have a pleasant sense of patronising him, when you condescend so far as to let him turn somersets; literal or literary, for your royal delight?'   Quite true: professional jesting lowers a man, and to describe you as a funny fellow, and nothing more, may be the truth, but it is not the whole truth.   That you are a humorist, and a humorist of the first water, none will deny.   I take it that *The Autocrat of the Breakfast Table* is one of the most genuinely humorous books written by any living author.   Yet I think there is more than mere humour in it.   Let us see.   Says the Autocrat, in illustrating the helplessness of men: 'Do you want an image of the human will or the self-determining principle, as compared with its pre-arranged and impassable restrictions?—A drop of water imprisoned in a crystal; you may see such a one in any mineralogical collection. One little fluid particle in the crystalline prism of the solid universe.' It could hardly be better put. There is something there beyond the reach of most humorists. Again, 'I find the great thing in this world is not so much where we stand, as in what direction we are moving. To reach the port of Heaven, we must sail sometimes with the wind and sometimes against it, but we must sail, and not drift, nor lie at anchor. There is one very sad thing in old friendships, to every mind which is moving onward. It is this: that one cannot help using his early friends, as the seaman uses the log, to mark his progress.' Those depths were never fathomed by the professional 'funny man.' Nor did he ever give such specimens of condensation as these: 'Every real thought on every subject knocks the wind out of somebody or other.' 'Sin has many tools, but a lie is the handle which fits them all.' And so I might go on multiplying instances to the confusion of Mr. Sala, and of all others who look on you as a mere humorist.

Mr. Haweis is nearer the mark in saying that 'Holmes is one of the few survivors of that chosen band of native thinkers and writers who have created American literature. . . . To the pleasures of money they have added the pleasures of imagination ; to the glories of trade and commerce they brought the worship of nature, the gift of the seeing eye, the sensitive heart, the uplifted soul.' There is no exaggeration there. You are a good deal more than a jester; you are a thinker, as every writer must be who is to do more than satisfy a passing need, or pander to a peculiar craze for the sake of the wages. Moreover, you are a charming poet and an effective story-teller. Not that I would place you in the very front rank among Transatlantic writers, either as a poet or a novelist. Criticism is nothing at all if it be not honest, and my conscience compels me to give you only a second place in either class. One must not forget that among the divine singers of America are Whittier and Lowell, and among its story-tellers Hawthorne and Poe. It is difficult to stand beside any one of the quartet without feeling more or less overshadowed. I dare say you would be the last man in the world to claim equality with the author of *The Scarlet*

Letter and *The House of the Seven Gables* on the one hand, or with the author of *Snow-Bound* and *Home Ballads and Poems* on the other. Whittier seems to me one of the truest and greatest sons of song whom this century has produced ; and, in his own line, Hawthorne is, in many respects, unrivalled. It will be a long time, I fear, before we get another *Scarlet Letter*. It is, in my estimation, the masterpiece of American literature, so far, and it remains a masterpiece in the literature of the world.

I do not think that so much could truthfully be said of anything you have done in fiction. You have not gone down into the deep places of the soul as Hawthorne has done. Yet you have touched some very deep springs, and shown that when you concentrate yourself you can not only be pathetic, but tragic ; you can not only draw tears, but you can paint that misery which is beyond the reach and the region of tears. There are parts of *Elsie Venner*, that marvellous romance of destiny, in which the tragedy is as strong as most readers would care to have it, and stronger than many could bear. Elsie is a wonderful, a powerful, and a telling study, which,

were it not for its pathological element, would
rank with the very best in the fiction of this
generation. 'Was Elsie Venner, poisoned by
the venom of a crotalus before she was born,
morally responsible for the volitional aberra-
tions which, translated into acts, become what is
known as sin, and, it may be, what is punished
as crime?' The question is an interesting and
pertinent one, but in trying to answer it you
make art suffer at the hand of science. Hawthorne, as you have yourself noticed, has a somewhat similar study in *The Marble Faun*, and
he, likewise, with all his penetration and imagination, fails. Indeed, his failure is signal.
There is confusion ; the elements of character,
which he endeavours to combine, are too diverse
to coalesce in one congruous and artistic whole.
The fact is, such studies are properly outside
the scope of art. It is not really the province
of art to meddle with inherited disease ; and
you, in doing it, were acting more in your scientific than in your artistic capacity. The novelist
had not quite mastered the doctor. The greatest
creations of genius are not founded on insanity.
Is Hamlet mad, think you? If he is, or was,

his madness had a great deal of method in it. Ophelia was mad, and so was Lear; but Shakespeare is careful in both cases to show it was the world, and not inherited disease, that had brought on their insanity. So much said, however, one would be hard to please who cavilled much at *Elsie Venner.* As a story I do not think the artistic blemish to which I have referred at all mars its interest. Nay, to many, I dare say, it will be an additional source of interest to watch the mental and physical paroxysms of the doomed girl—doomed through no fault of her own, but through a prenatal occurrence in which she had no share except in its consequence. One feels acutely for Elsie. She is a terrible study, and yet there is something soft and lovable in her. Hard, solitary, and self-centred as she seems, her heart did once go out to a fellow-being; but, alas! the love, which was truly a passion, was not returned, and Elsie curls up within herself again, more dangerous to herself and all about her than ever before. When the reader finds that Bernard Langdon does not return the girl's affection, he feels instinctively that she is doomed. Her one chance

has miscarried, and there is nothing to look
forward to but a tragedy worse than death.
The other characters in *Elsie Venner* are livingly
drawn.   Dr. Kitterage is a fine old fellow; and
I should say that Mr. Silas Peckham, Principal
of the Apollinean Institute, is the meanest man
in American fiction.   Helen Darley is a sweet
creation, and makes a striking contrast to Elsie.

I should be disposed to think, however, that
of all the stories you have written that of Iris in
The Professor at the Breakfast Table would be
the favourite with the general reader.   It is very
simple, very unpretentious, very touching; true
in every line, every sentiment, and delightfully
humorous until the darkness begins to gather
at the close; then, like life when there is only
a backward prospect, it grows stern for a little,
only, however, to soften into tender beauty again
as the sun sinks.   The final impression is one
of peace and repose.   Certain of your critics
have found this 'the most delicate as well as
the most powerful' of your works; and that
opinion, while much admiring your other stories,
I am inclined, on the whole, to indorse.   It is
not so elaborate as *Elsie Venner* or *A Mortal*

Antipathy, but I think it is sweeter than either, and surpasses both in fulness and strength of purely human interest. Iris herself, though slightly sketched, is a charming creation, and she gains by her contact with the deformed little gentleman. The latter is a very pathetic character, especially in that little love-scene at the close. That speech of his when the divinity student comes to ask him if he is prepared for the future is one not to be forgotten. ' "I am *not* a man, sir," said the little gentleman—"I was born into this world the wreck of a man, and I shall not be judged with a race to which I do not belong. Look at this!" he said, and held up his withered arm—"see there!" and he pointed to his misshapen extremities. "Lay your hand here!" and he laid his own on the region of his misplaced heart. "I have known nothing of the life of your race. When I first came to consciousness, I found myself an object of pity or a sight to show. . . . My life is the dying pang of a worn-out race, and I shall go down alone into the dust, out of this world of men and women, without ever knowing the fellowship of the one or the love of the other.

I will not die with a lie rattling in my throat. If another state of being has anything worse in store for me, I have had a long apprenticeship to give me strength that I can bear it. I don't believe it, sir. I have too much faith for that."' In the midst of his speech Iris bends over him and kisses him—him who had never had a kiss or caress of affection since his mother had left him. '"Shall I pray with you?" said the divinity student, after a pause. A little before he would have said, "Shall I pray *for* you?" The Christian religion, as taught by its Founder, is full of *sentiment,* so we must not blame the divinity student if he was overcome by those yearnings of human sympathy which predominate so much more in the sermons of the Master than in the writings of His successors, and which have made the parable of the Prodigal Son the consolation of mankind, as it has been the stumblingblock of all exclusive doctrines.' And the divinity student prays, meekly trusting the crippled child of sorrow to the Infinite Parent who does not fail to smooth the way. Those who have yet to make your acquaintance I should advise to get the story of Iris and read it, as a piece of genuine and touching sentiment, as a piece, also, of genuine and delightful humour.

The qualities which distinguish a writer's prose must, of necessity, if he be true to himself, mark his poetry also. Both in prose and verse you are essentially the same—the same keen observer, the same humorous commentator, the same genial companion, the same sterling friend of humanity. As a poet and as a story-teller you have the same lightness of touch, the same fascinating method of pointing a moral and adorning a tale; in a word, you are yourself whatever you write; so that your poetry need not be gone into at any length here. This much let me say, however, that in your poetic attempts you are always a poet. It has been your happy fortune to be able to ignore your own counsel to the literary or poetic tyro :—

> ' Don't mind if the index of sense is at zero,
>   Use words that run smoothly, whatever they mean ;
>   Leander, and Lilian, and Lillibullero,
>   Are much the same thing in the rhyming machine.'

I think you have very emphatically falsified your own facetious dictum.

Perhaps nothing concerning you is more remarkable than the cheerful, hopeful philosophy which sustains you in the evening of life. You have always been a buoyant writer, and your buoyancy is no less evident now than it was half a century ago. I will not say that your spirits are as high at eighty as they were at thirty—that were an unreasonable thing to expect, but I will say that few writers of your years have ever shown themselves so sunny. In 'Before the Curfew' there is the inevitable note of sadness, but there is no wail such as we so often hear from octogenarians. You can anticipate the ringing of the curfew, the putting out of the fire, with that calmness which is, perhaps, the most beautiful characteristic of old age, as it is certainly the best reward of a long life. There is subdued pathos, but no repining; least of all is there any quarrelling with the inevitable.

> 'Not bedtime yet ! The full-blown flower
>   Of all the year—this evening hour—
>   With friendship's flame is bright ;
>   Life still is sweet, the heavens are fair,
>   Though fields are brown and woods are bare,
>   And many a joy is left to share
>   Before we say good-night !

And when, our cheerful evening past,
The nurse, long waiting, comes at last,
Ere on her lap we lie—
In wearied nature's sweet repose,
At peace with all her waking foes,
Our lips shall murmur ere they close,
Good-night ! and not good-bye.'

That is too beautiful for comment.

To Mr. JOHN RUSKIN.

Sir,—Not long ago I read an article in a popular monthly magazine, signed by a well-known American artist, which proved, to the writer's entire satisfaction, that the world is miserably mistaken in considering you a reliable authority on Art. Your claims as an Art critic he ridiculed most mercilessly, and, having laughed to his heart's content, he boldly proceeded to assault and battery. No iconoclast was ever half so sweeping and destructive as this ingenuous child of nature from the illimitable prairies of the great West. To say that he left you not a leg to stand on would be but feebly describing the completeness of his act of demolition. Not satisfied with simply knocking you down, he danced on you, pulverised you, as it were; and then, when the terrible work was done, he smiled the triumphant smile of a Roman gladiator viewing the gory corse of

JOHN RUSKIN.

an antagonist. I remember that he specially
singled out for ridicule that celebrated description of Turner's 'Slave Ship' in *Modern
Painters.* I had read that passage before reading the article of the artist, and was weak and
illiterate enough to think it magnificent. To
say the truth, I thought it a good deal better
than the picture it professed to describe, giving
rather what the painter might have had in his
mind's-eye, than what he succeeded in putting
on canvas. But it was no blemish to my mind
that it took more out of the picture than is
really in it; nay, its superb exaggeration made
it, to me, one of the finest pieces of work
in all our English literature—so fine, indeed,
did it seem to me that what must I do but
get it off by heart, like Byron's address to
the ocean, Portia's speech on the quality of
mercy, Burke's fantasy about Marie Antoinette,
De Quincey's description of a stage-coach, Carlyle's panegyric on the nobility of labour, and
such like passages, which are admired either for
beauty of diction, or loftiness and vigour of
thought. But after reading that magazine
article I felt as if I had been wasting my time

imbibing wrong ideas. The writer did not, indeed, deny your power as a rhetorician. He was so good as to acknowledge that you had a marvellous mastery over words ; that your gift of expression was in every way superb ; that you had great emotional fervour ; and, he supposed, a certain melody of style which captivated the ear. But he said that your gifts in the matter of style only made you the more unreliable as a guide to uneducated persons seeking some knowledge of Art ; and he went on to analyse your description of Turner's 'Slave Ship,' and to expose its fallacies. He asked, for instance,— and there was the scorn of victory in his tone,— how anything could lose itself 'in the hollow of the night'; and he showed that you had introduced your most admired passages, not for the sake of truth, but for the sake of alliteration. Finally, he said that as neither you nor Turner had ever seen the deep sea, either in storm or calm, you could not possibly know anything about it. You were both dealing with vague generalities which had as much to do with the ocean as with the desert or the mountain ; and you, as critic, were praising, as high excellences in the work of Turner, that which does not exist in reality, never did exist, and never can exist, so long as the laws of Nature remain what they are. This, as you may suppose, was staggering to one who had always thought that thoroughness and accuracy were the special features of your work. To be told that you were writing about things concerning which you were totally ignorant, was a blow from which I did not at once recover.

But more startling revelations were in store. Scarcely had I got over the confusion into which the Yankee artist had thrown me, when I chanced to read the report of a speech delivered to a provincial audience by a 'distinguished' member of the British Parliament. The honourable member had evidently just been making himself up in political economy, and, as ill fortune would have it, had read what you have to say on the 'dismal science.' He instantly fell foul of you, and, with that consummate art of which members of the British Parliament are masters, he entertained his auditors with witty remarks on your fantastic notions of what is good for the State, and—I write it with awe—your colossal ignorance. It was a great effort, and he carried the whole house with him. The speech, according to the reporters (who are always impartial and veracious), was pointed with 'screams of laughter' and 'roars of applause'—all, as you will understand, at your expense. You sneered at the principles of political economy as laid down by political economists, said the distinguished member of the House of Commons, and what were you, pray? 'A man who found fault with the smoke of factories, and who would abolish railways; a man who would rather see an old daub of a picture, for which no right-minded man would give three brass farthings, hanging against the wall of a picturesque ruin than ships laden with merchandise, or trains full of happy holiday people. Here was a political economist indeed! And yet this singular individual had taken it upon himself to correct Adam Smith—Adam Smith, ladies and gentlemen—the father and founder of the great science of political economy, and John Stuart Mill, than whom, ladies and gentlemen, a more acute intellect has never risen among the sons of men. And, not only that, but he has dared to laugh at our trusted leader —the man of the ages—the man whose name will be written in history beside that of the Cæsars and the Napoleons, the Ciceros and the Pitts. Ladies and gentlemen, you will scarcely believe it, but the person of whom I speak has likened that great man to a pair of bagpipes with steam drones (cries of "Shame!"). It is not only an insult to our trusted leader, but also to every member of the House of Commons, that first assembly of gentlemen in the world, to which I am proud to belong. I tell Mr. Ruskin to-night, that the world may get on without pictures, as it will get on without cranks, but it can never—I repeat never—get along without political economy, and the man who says otherwise speaks in crass and unpardonable ignorance.' And so the distinguished member of the first assembly of gentlemen in the world complacently exposed your fallacies as a political economist, as the American artist had exposed your fallacies as an Art critic.

Nor was I yet done with these shocks. A little later, while in conversation with a man of the world, who had the reputation of being sharp and shrewd, and of having a good head on his shoulders, I happened to mention your name. 'Ah, Ruskin,' said my friend; 'yes—not bad in some ways; gives fancy descriptions of scenery and old buildings, and pictures, and all that—but rather impracticable.'

These were three opinions of you which came upon me, one after another, so rapidly as to take away my breath, metaphorically speaking; and, though I emphatically dissent from them, I much fear they give on the whole a too accurate indication of the sentiments of your countrymen regarding you. The blindest can see that you are at variance with your age. Much of what you regard with love and reverence, your fellow-men regard with cold indifference, too often, indeed, with open and insolent scorn. Much of what they praise and cherish, you denounce with vehement indignation. Mere material prosperity, the seeking after sensual pleasure, vulgar and extravagant display—nearly everything, in short, in which this era delights you do not commend nor sympathise with, while the moral beauty which is holiness, the self-sacrifice, all that goes to make the hero in the old sense of that word which you admire, your contemporaries mostly laugh at. Pursy Britannia goes her own way, pursuing her own pleasures, content so long as she is pursy, leaving you like one preaching in the wilderness, or to an audience that has stopped its ears. After all your exertions people still prefer ices at Florian's and music by moonlight on the Grand Canal, and paper lamps and the English magazines at M. Onagaria's, to the lessons of St. Mark's or the Ducal Palace. Better days may come, but that is the temper now. With the fate of Venice staring us in the face, with the stern admonitions which you draw from the ruins of her greatness and her grandeur, we still pursue selfish and ignoble pleasure while we have the means; we close our ears and harden our hearts and tell our souls to eat, drink, and be merry, because our barns are full and our presses bursting with new wine. And, as we gaze on the crumbling walls of Venice, heedless of any moral, so we think on the punishment of Tyre as a just retribution for her sins, unmindful that we, who inherit the greatness of both, if we forget their example,

' may be led through prouder eminence to less pitied destruction.' If ever we awake to the lesson which the history of those old powers teaches, the credit, I think, will be mainly due to you.

In this century and England of ours, two men have risen pre-eminent above all others in their stern faith to themselves and duty—men who refused, with a heroism worthy of the primitive epochs of the world, to truckle to expediency or barter their talents in the market-place for silver and gold, and these only. One was Thomas Carlyle, the other is yourself. In an age which is too often flippant, ribald, and scoffing, an age in which the cynic and the sceptic reign alternately, as the humour is to doubt or to sneer, an age that thinks of the Deity as a serviceable subject, affording opportunity for sallies of wit or graceful decorations of the fancy —in such an age you two have planted yourselves on the Bible, and proclaimed to men, without fear or favour, that they must live or perish according as they regard its teachings. One can imagine each of you starting forth on his career with that grand old prayer of Milton's—

' And chiefly Thou, O Spirit, that dost prefer
  Before all temples the upright heart and pure,
  Instruct me, for Thou knowest; Thou from the first
  Wast present, and with mighty wings outspread,
  Dove-like sat'st brooding on the vast abyss,
  And mad'st it pregnant; what in me is dark
  Illumine; what is low raise and support;
  That to the height of this great argument
  I may assert eternal Providence,
  And justify the ways of God to men.'

Not a little singular it is to find so much of the ruling spirit of Puritanism reappearing two centuries after it was supposed to be completely dead and done with. There is no chance for Puritanism, as it existed in the days of Cromwell and Milton, to get itself re-established in our midst. England, we are told, would not tolerate it, because it is too narrow, too bigoted, too much addicted to psalm-singing, too old-fashioned. We want spaciousness of creed in these liberal days. We cannot bear restraint, for it would diminish our enjoyment; nor antiquated notions of eternal punishment, for they would imply that we were not progressive; so we cut ourselves loose from the past and take up doctrines that are at once easy and elegant. When one remembers what Puritanism once did

for England at a critical time, and through England for the world, one is almost inclined to
regret the vogue of that 'breadth' which can
so easily dispense with conviction and make
eternal life dependent on æsthetic tastes and
the ability to frame a syllogism.   Faith has
been replaced by intellect.   Man's reason,
which De Quincey called the most contemptible of all his faculties, has asserted itself, and
the finite has mastered the infinite.   There
is no longer any mystery.   Life and death are
scientifically accounted for, and explained ; and
man may take his ease amid his cushions and
his tawdry upholstery.   In life the victualler,
the tailor, and the cabinetmaker are the grand
essentials ; in death, the fashionable undertaker
will not fail to do his duty : he will provide a fit
coffin and a respectable number of mourning-
coaches, and the exit is decently accomplished.
Puritanism was made of sterner stuff than this,
and so were Carlyle and you its latest, and, alas !
its most hopeless apostles.

I have bracketed you with Carlyle because
you and he are associated in the popular mind,
because your aims are essentially the same, and

because you have called yourself his disciple.
But I do not mean to imply that you resemble
each other in mental constitution, that you are
of equal power, or have an equal chance of
literary immortality. Indeed, I think that you
cannot be properly compared, except in your
unswerving fidelity to all that is good and true,
and your hatred of all that is base and false.
You are a great writer, but you are not quite a
Carlyle. He had all your gifts, and more. But
perhaps I shall make myself clearer if I glance
very briefly at you separately.

Carlyle is no less distinguished by his imaginative force, than by his moral fervour. If
elements of power will make writings live, his
must long exist. Much, of course, depends on
the utility or inutility of a writer's doctrines, and
Carlyle's are not fashionable just now. But
there is that in his works which makes them
independent of doctrine and will preserve them
as literature. His philosophy may, or may not,
be the philosophy of the future; it is to be
feared, indeed, that unless the world changes
radically he will appeal as a teacher only to a
few; but his force cannot die, and his literary

influence will always be great, even should his moral influence be *nil.* A dull man may be a moral reformer, but Carlyle was a man of intuition, a poet—in short, a man of genius. As Emerson said of Goethe, he sees at every pore. He is always more interesting than his subject, and sheds light upon all he approaches, not merely the light of purely intellectual faculties, but the light of imagination. As you have yourself said, only imagination can make writings live. The taste may be as elegant as that of Chesterfield, the style as fine as that of Congreve; there may be wit, there may even be humour, but if there be not imagination the principle of life is wanting, and speedy death and oblivion may be looked for. No learning, no brilliancy, no analytical power will make up for the want of imagination. Carlyle has a most powerful and vivid imagination—if not creative, at least associative and penetrative. He has other qualities of greatness besides—unrivalled humour, the most tender pathos, the most scathing sarcasm. No historian has ever dared to mingle humour, pathos, and tragedy as he has mingled them. And he is equally great, whether depicting men or things. As a portrait-painter he is unsurpassed by any writer save Shakespeare alone. Consider how well you know his characters :—Mirabeau, Danton, Robespierre, Voltaire, Frederick the Great, Cromwell, Jeffrey, Cagliostro, Dr. Francia. He cannot touch on a character in the most casual way, without lighting it up. View him how you will, Carlyle is a Titan.

Now, while saying frankly that I consider you a man of genius, I should not be disposed to call you a Titan. As an interpreter of the symbolic meaning of what is best in Art you are unmatched. In that respect you are superior to Carlyle, who knew little of Art, as represented by pictures, and seemed not to value it at all. In his *Life of John Sterling*, and elsewhere, he speaks slightingly of it, calls it a windy doctrine, and insinuates that it is quite unworthy of the attention of any serious man. You have shown that, if rightly considered, it may well be studied by the best of men. This is your great merit. You have shown that pictures are not merely for the idler and the dilettante, but for earnest, serious men and women, who have sufficient

love and sympathy to perceive their hidden
meanings. And, then, as a descriptive writer
you occupy a quite, unique position. No other
writer has ever described the face of Nature
with such elaboration as you, nor transferred
to his pages so much of her warmth and colouring. There are parts of *Modern Painters* that
cannot be described save by the epithet 'gor-
geous.' Nor is this gorgeousness attained by
the exclusion of the mean and the common.
Milton found Paradise enchanting, but you go
to our meadows, among the grazing kine, and
preach your sermon from a blade of grass ; and
it is only the truth to say that a field of pasture
becomes as interesting as the bower of Eve.

It should not be forgotten, however, that, as
you have yourself said, minds of the very highest
order do not take much to descriptions of
scenery ; or, having taken to them, speedily
abandon them. Your work is scenic from first
to last. You have given us no portraits worth
naming beside Carlyle's. It may be you have
never seriously tried portrait-painting. But it
is doubtful whether you could have succeeded,
even if you had made the endeavour ; for you

seem to lack that sympathetic insight which marks the master of character. Perhaps it would be fatal to the moral teacher to be too widely sympathetic, yet Carlyle had as wide a sympathy with men as Shakespeare himself. You have not this sympathy, and therefore cannot exhibit it in a gallery of portraits.

Much is made of style in these days, and a writer's manner is often more looked to than his matter. Whatever may be said of you in other respects, no one will deny your unrivalled superiority as a stylist. Let me give one example of it. It is one which seems to have pleased yourself, and, therefore, may be quoted with fairness. I think I could give a more brilliant example, but I am glad to take what has the stamp of your own approval. It describes Venice :—

'A city of marble did I say? nay, rather a golden city, paved with emeralds. For, truly, every pinnacle and turret glanced or glowed, overlaid with gold or bossed with jasper. Beneath, the unsullied sea drew in deep breathing to and fro its eddies of green waves. Deep-hearted, majestic, terrible as the sea—the men of Venice moved in sway of power and war; pure as her pillars of alabaster stood her mothers and maidens; from foot to brow, all noble, walked her knights; the low bronzed gleaming of sea-rusted armour shot angrily under her blood-red mantle folds. Fearless, faithful, patient, impenetrable, implacable—every word a fate, sate her Senate. In hope and honour, lulled by flowing of wave around their isles of sacred sand, each with his name written and the cross graced at his side, lay her dead. A wonderful piece of world. Rather, itself a world. It lay along the face of the waters, no larger, as its captains saw it from their masts at evening, than a bar of sunset that could not pass away; but for its power, it must have seemed to them as if they were sailing in the expanse of heaven, and this a great planet, whose orient edge widened through ether. A world from which all ignoble care and petty thoughts were banished, with all the common and poor elements of life. No foulness, nor tumult, in those tremulous streets, that filled or fell beneath the moon; but rippled music of majestic change, or thrilling silence. No weak walls could rise above them ; no low-roofed cottage, nor straw-built shed. Only the strength as of rock, and the finished setting as of stones most precious. And around them, as far as the eye could reach, still the soft moving of stainless waters, proudly pure ; as not the flower, so neither the thorn nor the thistle could grow in the glancing fields. Ethereal strength of Alps, dream-like, vanish in high procession beyond the Torcellan shore ; blue islands of Paduan hills, poised in the golden west. Above, free winds and fiery clouds, raging at their will : brightness out of the north, and balm from the south, and the star of the evening and morning, clear in the limitless light of arched heaven and circling sea.'

As a gem of English, I do not think that could easily be beaten, even in the present era of stylists.

To Mr. JAMES RUSSELL LOWELL.

Sir,—When the critics find time hanging heavy on their hands, it is their handsome and pleasant fashion to fall foul of the age in which they live ; and this, it seems, is one of irredeemable mediocrity. According to our literary censors we have no great poems, no great plays, no great novels, no great histories, no great biographies—nothing great in fact except, perhaps, our pretensions, which, though vast enough in all conscience, are of little present value, and are certain to be quite worthless as drafts on posterity. It is a doleful and depressing view of the situation, and, I am inclined to think, a false and, therefore, an unfair one. As a creed, even when fallen back on only at odd times, pessimism is always bad—bad morally, æsthetically, financially ; nor does it mend matters that its dismal and depreciatory

54

JAMES RUSSELL LOWELL.

croakings have so often an aspect of truth.
Some one has aptly and truthfully observed
that it disenchants and ungifts us; and whatever does that had better be avoided; so that
as a question of policy a cheerful self-con-
fidence, a buoyant self-esteem, a tendency to
exaggeration on the score of our own merits,
despite the danger there may be from vanity,
are, on the whole, healthy and hopeful signs.
To say the truth, only the hopeless faultfinder
would seriously deny that this age, though the
butt of so much pleasant ridicule, the theme for
so much ingenious depreciation, is as respect-
ably equipped in the matter of literary talent as
most of the ages that have gone before it.
To be sure it is neither Augustan nor Eliza-
bethan; but it might be shown that we
have still some tolerable writers in both
prose and verse; some writers whose works
will outlast this generation; and more than
one whose writings, if I have any critical
judgment, will go to permanently adorn and
enrich that treasury of English literature which,
after all our conquests and gains, remains the
grandest possession of the Anglo-Saxon race.

Nothing is more amusing than man's constant readiness to abuse the age in which he lives and extol the ages that are past. We all know —at any rate all of us who are gifted with imagination, that the past is, in all respects, unmatchably glorious. A golden haze overhangs it, different altogether from the crude, cold, grey atmosphere of the present. The apples of the past were all grown in the garden of the Hesperides; they had a richer coat and a more delicious flavour than the common baldwins and russets of to-day. The poetry of the past was all indited in delectable grottoes and fragrant bowers and arbours and on the daisied banks of limpid and purling brooks; and it is only fair to assume that the printers' ink was tinted with gold and mixed with rosewater. The romance of the past was real romance, not simulated like ours. There were dryads, and naiads, and shepherdesses in the past, while the present possesses only matrons, young ladies, and old maids. To be sure, men complained in the past. But we wisely take no notice of that, well knowing their querulousness was caused by a superfluity of the delectable things

of life. Men complain, now, with reason. As
the poet says—

> ‘ Here is Hades, manifest, beholden
>   Surely, surely here, if aught be sure.’

Yet, though we cannot compete with the past,
that does not seem a sufficient reason for
abusing the present.

Seriously in a literary way, at least, the
present age has no reason to be ashamed of
itself. If it has no Shakespeares, nor Miltons,
it has, at least, its Drydens and its Popes. The
Era that produces ‘ The Ring and the Book,’
‘ In Memoriam,’ ‘ Snowbound,’ and ‘ The Vision
of Sir Launfal,’ may hold up its head beside
even the classic age of Queen Anne, an age
which, in my estimation, has received rather
more than its due meed of praise. Instead of
bemoaning our condition, as if only cowards
and dotards were generated nowadays, it is
better to believe with yourself that

> ‘ Here ’mid the bleak waves of our life and care,
>   Float the green fortunate Isles
>   Where all the hero-spirits dwell and share
>   Our martyrdoms and toils ;
>   The present moves attended
>   With all of brave and excellent and fair
>   That made the old time splendid.’

However, it is not now my business to render justice to the ages, but to set down, with what brevity and clearness I may, my opinions of the creator of ' Hosea Biglow.' I mention Hosea especially, because it is to him rather than to your more ambitious or more serious works that you owe your vogue.

Of the *Biglow Papers*, then, which first gained you recognition, and by which you are still known to the majority, I find Mr. Thomas Hughes writing as follows: ' For real unmistakable genius—for that glorious fulness of power which knocks a man down at a blow for sheer admiration, and then makes him rush into the arms of the knocker-down, and swear eternal friendship with him for sheer delight, the *Biglow Papers* stand alone.' The *Biglow Papers* do certainly stand alone, at all events they do not so closely resemble any other production as to give the idea of imitation. Mr. Hughes finds that if you resemble any of the satirists it is Jean Paul Richter. With that verdict, however, I cannot concur. Glimpses and suggestions of Jean Paul you may give (a man of your extensive reading could hardly help picking up ideas from other minds), but it seems to me that as a satirist you are much more strongly under Scottish than German influence. I think that if you had a model at all in your satire it was Burns. Indeed, my impression is that the original idea of the *Biglow Papers*, at any rate so far as their form is concerned, came to you through reading the works of the Scottish ploughman. Burns is a standing example of what genius can do with dialect. He was the first writer of real power to adopt, in all its fulness and simplicity, the common speech of the peasantry, which in his hands is graceful and fluent, and for potency unrivalled. It may be that his example set you to work in the vein which has yielded so much rich ore. Nor in such cases is it any discredit to be a borrower. So long as the borrower makes good use of what he takes he is fairly within his rights in borrowing. Skakespeare is the greatest writer, and the greatest borrower of whom the world has any knowledge. And could we wish that he had borrowed less? Surely not. He takes things in such a princely way, and makes such splendid use of them, that we would fain see him take more. And if you have taken a hint from Burns, you certainly have made such use of it as only genius can. The *Biglow Papers*, notwithstanding their smack of Burns, are really unique. One of your critics finds their characteristics to be 'the most exuberant and extravagant humour, coupled with strong, noble, Christian purpose—a thorough scorn for all that is false and base, all the more withering because of the thorough geniality of the writer . . . every word tells, every laugh is a blow; as if the good Momus had turned out as Mars, and were hard at work fighting every inch of him, grinning his broadest all the while.' It is hard to say whether the wit, the humour, the satire, the philosophy, or the Christianity of the *Biglow Papers* is the more admirable. Certainly they are all there at their best; all working, and working successfully in the cause of humanity. But I prefer to consider the work as a contribution to literature, rather than as an effort in philanthropy. The cause you advocated has been won, after such a struggle as the world never before witnessed; but your writings remain, and, I think, will long remain as a piece of literature.

In the first blush of pleasure on reading anything so fresh and racy, so humorous and so caustic, so popular and yet so profound, as the *Biglow Papers*, one is apt to exaggerate merits. Yet it would be hard to employ epithets regarding the best parts of that work which could not be justified on the strictest critical grounds. The final test of all true merit is intellect. When you say that there is intellect in any work, you give it almost the highest possible praise. The *Biglow Papers* show the stamp of an acute and capacious mind. One reads with the deepening impression that, had you cared, you could have done anything else equally well. ' I have no idea of a great man,' says Carlyle, in his emphatic way, ' who could not be anything he pleased.' And assuredly it is no flattery to say that you give one the impression of that power and adaptability which the sage of Chelsea had in his mind's-eye. Hosea Biglow and Bird o' Fredum Sawin would be excellent politicians—minus their consciences ; and the Rev. Homer Wilbur, A.M., is a very sound philosopher, in his old-fashioned way.

It is the fate of all-eminent humorists to have their one gift prized at the expense of all other gifts they may possess. Your humour is so abounding that it diverts the attention from your other qualities. Every one is conscious of your power to raise a laugh, but not every one, in their glee at being so well entertained, what there is in addition to the humour. For instance, in that keen and cutting satire, 'The Pious Editor's Creed,' most readers find more amusement than food for reflection ; yet there is a deeper intent than to amuse. There is a terrible grimness, a terrible earnestness behind the laughter. It is rather Hercules with his club than Momus with his grin that the clarified vision will behold. I am not sure that since ' Holy Willie's Prayer ' was written we have had anything more severe than that ' Pious Editor's Creed.' Were it not for its humour, it is enough to make *American* editors squirm in their chairs for ever.

Almost equally severe are your pictures of the avaricious, time-serving politician, the man

without patriotism, without morality, without a
single worthy motive, a single ambition above
place and the emoluments and perquisites per-
taining to it—the man who, whatever trouble
his country may be in, is always found ' frontin'
north by south.'   Then, in the broader phases
of humour, hardly anything could be more
mirth-provoking than such pieces as ' What Mr.
Robinson Thinks,' and ' The Epistles of Bird o'
Fredum Sawin.'   In Mr. Sawin there is a jovial
spirit, which even prison walls and broken ribs,
and loss of arms and legs, cannot damp.   When
he loses a lower limb, he is not without consolation in his loss :—

' There 's one good thing though to be said about my
    wooden new one.
  The liquor can't get into it ez't used to in the true
    one ;
  So it saves drink,'

which is certainly a consideration to one whose
thirst is perennial and whose dollars are limited.
And in jail his jocularity is still unabated.   He
apologises for his gross unpunctuality as a cor-
respondent by stating that he is—

> ' Where sech things ez paper 'n ink air clean agin the
>   rules,
> A kind o' vicy varsy house built dreffle strong and
>   stout,
> So 'st honest people can't git in, nor t' other sort git
>   out.
> An' with the winders so contrived, you 'd prob'ly like
>   the view
> Better a-lookin' in than out, though it seems singular,
>   tu ;
> But then the landlord sets by ye, can't bear ye out o'
>   sight,
> And locks ye up ez reg'lar as an outside door at night.'

And no one will deny that correspondence is difficult, and apt to be irregular under such circumstances. But Mr. Sawin has a heart and spirit above all the ills of fate, and can laugh whatever betide.

In some parts of the *Biglow Papers* the humour is so audacious that some good and worthy people have thought it verged on irreverence. For example, where Hosea insists on personal responsibility for killing one's fellow-creatures :—

> ' If you take a sword an' dror it,
>   An' go stick a feller thru,
> Guv'ment ain't to answer for it,
>   God 'll send the bill to you.'

And again, where he says :—

> 'Ye 'll hev' to git up airly
> If ye want to take in God.'

Certain Christian people, I say, mistaking your motive in writing such lines, have taken exception to the familiar use of the name of the Deity. But it is only a plain statement of a great and weighty truth ; and your own explanation is ample when you state 'that one of the things I am proud of in my countrymen is that they do not put their Maker away far from them, or interpret the fear of God into being afraid of Him . . . and when people stand in great dread of an invisible power, I suspect they mistake quite another personage for the Deity.' Those who brought the charge of profanity had not understood the spirit in which you wrote, nor the lesson you wished to inculcate. But there are always pious people to retard reforms and misapprehend the intentions of authors.

I have dwelt long on the *Biglow Papers*, yet I cannot quit them without noting one or two of the pregnant sayings of the Rev. Homer Wilbur. In the superabundance of humour and satire, Mr. Wilbur and his trenchant truths are apt to be forgotten. That ‘Table Talk’ of his, short as it is, is excellent, as good in its way as the table talk of Samuel Johnson. The following are, I think, worthy of being stored in the memory :—‘There is no impiety so abject as that which expects to be dead-headed through life, and which, calling itself Trust in Providence, is in reality asking Providence to trust us, and take up all our goods on false pretences.’ ‘Unless one’s thoughts pack more neatly in verse than in prose, it is wiser to refrain. Commonplace gains nothing by being translated into rhyme, for it is something which no hocus-pocus can transubstantiate with the real presence of living thought.’ ‘Beware of simulated feeling, it is hypocrisy’s first cousin.’ ‘There seem, nowadays, to be two sources of literary inspiration—fulness of mind and emptiness of pocket.’ ‘Attention is the stuff that memory is made of, and memory is accumulated genius.’ ‘Do not look for the Millennium as imminent. One generation is apt to get all the wear it can out of the old clothes of the last, and is always sure to use up every paling of the old fence that will hold a nail in building the new.'

Your serious poems—the poems by which, I dare say, you would wish to be remembered—still remain to be noticed. They are not all of equal merit, and perhaps none is quite Miltonic. But they are one and all true poems—that is, they are not prose and commonplace, perked, cramped, and squeezed into rhyme. They are not a mere rhetorical jingle, like so much which at present passes current for poetry. They are instinct with fire, and they are full of imagination. It would be a great pleasure to me did space permit, which it doesn't, to dilate on their qualities. I think you are one of the most useful and satisfying of modern poets. For the growing mind wishing to imbibe right ideas of men and things, I know not, among living writers, your superior. Wherefore I should like to dwell at length on the lessons you teach I should like to look through that 'Fable for Critics,' and that delightful ode, 'To a Dandelion,' and 'The Vision of Sir Launfal,' and 'Heart's-ease and Rue,' where your muse is in her mellow Indian summer (long may it be ere her winter come), and many other pieces; but I may not.

However, as I have indulged myself by transcribing some specimens of your writing in a comic and satirical vein, I cannot forbear to quote one of your sonnets, which shows you in a different light. It shows that the true poet, the true man indeed, must, in spite of himself, be sometimes serious. It is the sonnet 'To the Spirit of Keats.'

'Great Soul, thou sittest with me in my room,
   Uplifting me with thy vast quiet eyes,
   On whose full orbs with kindly lustre lies
The twilight warmth of ruddy ember-gloom;
Thy clear, strong tones will oft bring sudden bloom
   Of hope secure to him who lonely cries,
   Wrestling with the young poet's agonies,
Neglect and scorn, which seem a certain doom;
   Yes, the few words which, like great thunder-drops,
Thy large heart down to earth shoots doubtfully;
   Thrilled by the inward lightning of its might,
   Serene and pure like gushing joy of light,
Shall track the eternal chords of destiny
   After the moon-led pulse of ocean stops.'

Of your prose works it is hardly necessary to speak, for I believe they are even better known than your poetry. They display that humour and insight which distinguish your poems. Moreover, they reveal a scholarship for which your poems would hardly prepare one. As a critic, perhaps, your chief characteristic is sanity. Your essays on Dryden, Chaucer, Dante, and Keats, are masterpieces. That on Carlyle is not so satisfactory ; but in his case there is some excuse, for the grim old man had irritated you by his attitude on American questions during the Civil War. There is an asperity, too, in the paper ' On a Certain Condescension in Foreigners,' which is unusual with you. But here, again, you had, as your countrymen say, been rubbed ' agin the fur.'

To COUNT LYOF NIKOLAEVICH TOLSTOI.

Monsieur le Comte,—When the late Matthew Arnold wrote that 'the Russian novel has now the vogue and deserves to have it: if fresh literary productions maintain this vogue and enhance it we shall all be learning Russian,' he was for once in his life clearly and emphatically giving voice to the popular sentiment. It is really not improbable that we shall presently be learning your language in order to study your works; for we are a peculiar people, and think no labour too great that is undertaken in honour of a favourite. Nay, if you are reasonable, and do not expect too much of us, it may be that in a lackadaisical way even your rather singular doctrines may become fashionable amongst us. Of late years you have dealt a good deal in theology, and theology is generally supposed to be dry reading; but you must

LEO TOLSTOI.

not suppose, M. le Comte, that we dislike theology. On the contrary, we delight, we revel, in it. For instance, no novel is so popular with us as the theological novel. Ladies courageously write this class of fiction, and other ladies quite cheerfully take it to their boudoirs, and puzzle their fair heads over its recondite passages in preference to going to study the fashions at the opera ; statesmen turn aside from affairs of state to write articles on it ; clergymen take it into the pulpit with them and preach sermons on it to enraptured audiences ; merchants discuss it after 'change; lawyers, oddly enough, grow casuistical over it—in a word, it is immensely popular. There is little danger therefore of our being offended with the theological foibles of any favourite writer. Only, as I have already hinted, you must not expect us to follow you too far. The line must be drawn when our material interests are touched. As you are perhaps aware, we are a practical people, and you must see yourself how extremely inconvenient it would be to put your charming theories into practice. We shall be quite content to discuss them, and watch how they suc-

ceed experimentally in autocratic Russia. When
there has been a general distribution of property
in that free and enlightened country we will
give the matter graver consideration here. It
is fit that reform, like charity, should begin at
home.

As a writer you were lucky in making your
appearance at a most opportune moment. 'A
pigmy's a giant,' says our Mr. Meredith, 'if he
can manage to arrive in season'; and though
you are far from being a pigmy, there is an
obvious advantage even to you in arriving at a
time when there was a general search for novelty.
When you were discovered (an author never
makes himself known, but is always discovered)
our appetites were sorely cloyed; we were
languid and sick, inexpressibly bored with the
endless imitations of the grotesque horseplay
and free-weeping of Dickens, the ugly cynicism
of Thackeray, and the heavy tragedy of George
Eliot. We needed an alterative, and no alterative was to be had. We turned our longing
faces to the great West and were disappointed.
Mr. Henry James, though extremely neat and
precise and well-bred, is a trifle chilly. Mr.

Howells is too much afraid of the big passions, and Mr. Bret Harte is repeating himself unconscionably. To France we scarcely durst look lest our characters might suffer. M. Zola is really a shocking man, and M. Daudet is hardly so circumspect as he might be (at any rate so we were told), and, being piously credulous in such matters, we sighed and passed on. Germany, Italy, and Spain we found almost barren, and we were just on the point of abandoning the weary search, when lo ! we saw three amorphous figures looming on the steppes of Russia. We hurried thither, and immediately there was a sensation. We pounced on Turgueneff, then on Dostoieffsky ; and now we are struggling with yourself—surveying you on all sides, taking your dimension, and giving you an occasional crack and thump to see whether or no you sound hollow. The majority of us have not yet quite made up our minds regarding you. Nor need this be a surprise, for to the uncritical you are a most tantalising phenomenon. You bear no trace of familiar influence. You belong to neither the romantic nor the naturalistic school as established in our midst. You are not a bowwowist nor a 'dismal conceited analyst.' Your philosophy is not the philosophy of Robert Elsmere, nor of Professor Huxley, nor of M. Renan. There is no evidence that you know anything at all of the sharp divisions set up between our several schools of fiction. What is the stolid Briton, as fond of his prejudices as of his roast-beef, to make of you? Obviously he can only stare and ejaculate, and turn you over, thinking what manner of man you can be, and praying you may not turn out a monster. That is the attitude towards you of the average British reader.

But, as already stated, there are others even in Britain who recognise in you those qualities which constitute a bond of brotherhood between men of all ages and of all climes. You are no partisan, you belong to no clique or coterie—you could not if you would ; for as a man, by taking thought, cannot add one inch to his stature, neither can a really great soul narrow himself so as to become the creature of a sect. You have the breadth and the courage of greatness. In your fidelity to nature you sometimes remind one of Shakespeare and sometimes of Scott and sometimes of Cervantes and sometimes of Balzac. Their work may not always be pleasant, but it is always true, and therefore always great. They are as unflinching as Nature herself, and will not be turned aside for fear of giving offence to the goody-goody—that saccharine compound of inanities and ineptitudes which is at present threatening to take all the savour out of life. You, like the great ones I have named, deal with vice and crime, with fierce and sinful passions, with a fine impartiality quite unexampled in a time when so many of our writers are tremulously pious and mealy-mouthed, and so many more are vauntfully immoral. You do not go in search of the base and the ugly, like some of the prurient writers of France and their imitators in America, nor do you absolutely shun them, like some of our Sunday-school authors in England, who will not so much as mention the devil except by some polite and veiling appellative. Wickedness stands in your way, and you touch on it, as every writer must who is not a moral coward ; but you never make sin engaging, and you never fail to note its consequences. As

Matthew Arnold well said, you do not pay homage to the Goddess Lubricity.

As a novelist you are generally classed among the realists. Arbitrary classification is perhaps necessary in criticism, but it is misleading. When realism is mentioned in England we instantly think of M. Zola and yourself; and though I am far from holding the conventional British opinion of the inexorable author of *L'Assommoir*, I believe the association does you a clear injustice. You have just as little and as much in common with M. Zola as with Walter Scott and Victor Hugo. As a matter of fact you are one of the writers (too few alas !) who cannot be satisfactorily classed. If we take *War and Peace*, for instance, it is difficult to decide whether romance or realism predominates. Both are there in the highest and best sense. The realism is as faithful as the best of Jane Austen, the romance as fine as the best of Nathaniel Hawthorne ; and in combination they produce a result which is perhaps unparalleled in the later literature of the world. *War and Peace* is an unmatchable book, a book which demonstrates the foolishness of critical canons, and the futility of arbitrary classifications.

In such sketches as 'the death of Ivan Ilyitch,' you are purely and simply, I had almost said atrociously, realistic. I know no piece of writing of equal length so exquisitely gruesome as that sombre study of the insidious progress of disease, and the blighting of a great ambition. It is a study so absorbing that when you begin to read you cannot stop till the end is reached, and so painful, indeed so hideous, that you seem to move in an atmosphere of disease and death long after closing the book. There, M. le Comte, you give unadulterated realism, and there is no difficulty as to class, but in your larger works you are quite as much the poet as the analyst ; and it is unsafe and unsatisfactory to relegate you to any particular category. The most comprehensive label will give but a dim and confused idea of your genius and qualities.

And, indeed, why should we give ourselves unnecessary trouble, and do you a gratuitous injustice by affixing any label ? Is it not given to intelligent men in this nineteenth century to enjoy and admire without being scientifically concerned regarding that which yields them pleasure? Would it not be feasible, for instance, to say that *War and Peace*, or *Anna Karenin*, is a great work without being painfully or misleadingly argumentative in support of the statement? Is it absolutely necessary to say this part is idyllic, this realistic, that again soundly philosophic, that well reasoned, that analytic, that romantic? Must we dissect afresh, and pass a *cultured* judgment on every character we encounter? Must we, with laboured and pedantic phraseology, go into the good and bad qualities of Pierre Besuskof, of Andrew Bolkonsky, of Helen, of Natacha Rostow, of Kiva, of Ivan Ilyitch, of Zhilin, of Prince Basil? Must we take the gigantic canvas of *War and Peace* to bits and examine each under the microscope? It surely is not necessary at this time of day. At any rate, for myself, I would make the simple confession that I think *War and Peace* and *Anna Karenin* two of the few really great novels of the world?—say two of the first dozen; or shall we stretch a point and say two of the first score? That they easily place you among the giants is, I think, beyond all question. You take your place in that illustrious front rank with Walter Scott and Goethe and Hugo and Balzac and Cervantes and George Sand, an immortal while still in the flesh.

But it is a significant indication of our national tastes, and the bent of our national genius, that it is not as a novelist you interest us most. Pre-eminent as you are in the art of writing fiction, it is rather as a theologian and moral philosopher that you occupy our attention. We read with avidity, and discuss with solemnity, those very remarkable works of yours setting forth your religious beliefs, and your views on certain portions of Scripture. I have already said that theology interests us most profoundly; and it is only stating a simple fact to say that many who do not know your novels, or care little for them, are deeply moved by your religious writings. Perhaps it is because they have rather more freshness and originality than is usual in theological works. It may not, indeed, seem a very original thing to aspire to follow the teachings of Jesus. For close on twenty centuries the whole Christian world has been persuading itself that its conduct has, in the main, conformed to the commands of Christ. Wherein then do your doctrines differ from those of the rest of mankind? In denying that there was anything figurative in the sermons and other addresses — public and private—of Jesus. Christians—even the most devout and sincere—have been wont to cross great difficulties and chasms by the easy bridge of figurativeness. It would be quite impossible to literally obey such and such a command, they say. Jesus did not mean us to perform impossibilities, therefore that particular part must be figurative. You answer 'No; it is not figurative—nothing that Christ ever spoke was figurative. Every utterance of his was as direct and precise as language could make it. Jesus meant you to obey his commands *literally.* If you choose to make a plain injunction figurative you do so at your peril. Jesus meant all he said.' And to make the matter clearer you formulated your belief in five commandments.

1st.—'Live in peace with all men—treat no one as contemptible and beneath you. Not only allow yourself no anger, but do not rest until you dissipate even unreasonable anger in others against yourself.'

2d.—'No libertinage and no divorce: let every man have one wife and every woman one husband.'

3d.—'Never on any pretext take an oath of service of any kind; all such oaths are imposed for a bad purpose.'

4th.—'Never employ force against the evil-doer; bear whatever wrong is done you without opposing the wrongdoer or seeking to have him punished.'

5th.—'Renounce all distinction of nationality; do not admit that men of another nation may ever be treated by you as enemies; love all men alike as alike near to you; do good to all alike.'

It must be admitted that you support your interpretation of the Gospels with very considerable force of logic, and that in the course of your inquiries you shed light on many obscure passages of Scripture. You go to the fountain-head, and are hardly civil to Biblical Commentators. You find them all blinded by tradition, you say, not one of them to be relied on ; and then you write this terrible sentence—‘ I firmly believe that, a few centuries hence, the history of what we call the scientific activity of this age will be a prolific subject for hilarity and pity.’ Ah ! M. le Comte, how unkind of you, considering the vast number of religious and theological writers who have used their talents and their learning in leading us easily over thorny places ! You are indeed a disturbing phenomenon ; we were at peace, and you would not let us alone ; we were pleased to exercise the imagination regarding the doctrine of Jesus, and you say that imagination must be rigidly excluded.

And then think, M. le Comte, what you bid us do. ‘ Our entire social fabric,’ you say, ‘ is founded upon principles that Jesus reproved.’ Has our civilisation been indeed then a failure, and are we to make a fresh start ? Are we to dismiss the constable, the magistrate, and the executioner ? Are we to open the prison doors and let the whole corrupt mass of humanity that seethes within flow out and invade our homes ? Is the thief to be allowed to put forth his hand and steal with impunity? Is the murderer to take life, and the libertine to debauch virtue without let or hindrance? Are we to divide our property with the idle and profligate, and toil for those who oppress us? Is the Church to give up her tithes, and must rulers forego their well-earned rewards? Is there to be no distinction between man and man, except in power to benefit others? Are we, in a word, to undo all that civilisation—that great progressive cumulative force which has been the theme of such frequent laudation from the ablest and best of the sons of men—are we to undo all that it has done? And you answer, yes,—most emphatically, yes; and as your authority give, 'The Sermon on the Mount.' But was the Sermon on the Mount ever preached? Mr. Huxley doubts it; and he doubts also whether 'the so-called Lord's Prayer was ever prayed by Jesus of Nazareth.' What then, M. le Comte, if your doctrine of Jesus is not the doctrine of Jesus at all, but something attributed to him by fable? In that case, would not your whole theological super-structure collapse? But whatever may be your fate as a theologian, I think that as an artist there can be but one opinion concerning you —namely, that you are 'a great soul and a great writer,' and that your place in universal literature is secure.

JAMES ANTHONY FROUDE.

To Mr. JAMES ANTHONY FROUDE.

Sir,—You are known in the five-fold character of historian, biographer, novelist, essayist, and writer of travels. That you should have attempted so much proves that you are a man of more than ordinary courage; that you have acquitted yourself so well in each of these widely dissimilar *rôles* shows that you are a man of more than ordinary capacity. It is not, perhaps, within the scope of human talent to be at once various and supreme in excellence. The Admirable Crichtons of whom we occasionally hear are, I suspect, rather fables than facts, stimulating creations of the imagination, and no more to be treated as verities than Don Quixote, or Baron Munchausen, or the Count of Monte Cristo. At any rate one never meets them in real life. And, indeed, though versatility is a good thing, it is not without its disadvantages. Its achievements are specious rather than solid, and rarely add to the world's stock of knowledge, or enhance the world's comfort. One admires the easy adaptability of Proteus, and the handiness of Briareus in carrying on many occupations simultaneously, but Hercules with only two stout arms and an unchangeable shape did more meritorious service than either. Folks like that vicar of whom Praed sings that—

> ' His talk is like a stream which runs,
>   With rapid change, from rocks to roses ;
>   It slips from politics to puns,
>   It glides from Mahomet to Moses ;
>   Beginning with the laws that keep
>   The planets in their radiant courses,
>   And ending with some precept deep
>   For skinning eels or shoeing horses '—

though highly interesting and brilliant individuals, are in the main only a species of human fire rockets that may for a little dazzle, but can hardly benefit mankind. It remains mostly true what the philosophic Mr. Pope long ago asserted, that—

> ' One science only will one genius fit,
>   So wide is art, so narrow human wit.'

Or as the German Shakespeare has it : ' We

should guard against a talent which we cannot
hope to practise in perfection. Improve it as
we may, we shall always, in the end, when the
merit of the master has become apparent to us,
painfully lament the loss of time and strength
devoted to such botching.'

Now while it would be most unjust to aver
that you have ever botched anything you have
attempted, it is no more than the truth to say
that in hardly any work you have accomplished
have you shown yourself an impeccable artist.
Some critics, indeed, have fallen foul of your
entire series of works, and condemned them in
one sweeping sentence. Those astute persons
inform us that, as an historian, you are so full of
inveterate prepossessions, that your presenta-
tions of men and things have little value,
that as a biographer you are careless, and as a
writer of travels almost unprecedentedly inac-
curate. On the latter point, indeed, they claim
living witnesses. The Australians and New
Zealanders, for instance, are said to repudiate
your descriptions of themselves and their coun-
tries, to aver that you rarely took the trouble to
observe things for yourself, and that when you

tried you were not successful. 'And how,' demand your critics triumphantly, 'are we to depend on the historical statements of a man who cannot describe what he has seen with his own eyes?' The question is pertinent, for it seems no more than reasonable to doubt the reliability of the historian who cannot tell us the exact aspect of things he has himself looked upon. Into the question whether you are right or wrong regarding the Antipodes, however, I will not now enter; for I have seen so little of the land of the kangaroo myself that it would ill become me to question the correctness of your observations concerning it; only it might be remarked that if you are right respecting it, most other travellers, from the late Anthony Trollope, and Mr. George Augustus Sala, and Mr. Archibald Forbes, and Dr. Dale down, are wrong. But your historical and biographical work is another matter, and on that I may be allowed an opinion like the rest of your critics.

Macaulay, in one of his most brilliant essays, informs us that 'History, at least, in its state of ideal perfection, is a compound of poetry and philosophy. It impresses general truths on the mind by a vivid representation of particular characters and incidents. But, in fact, the two hostile elements of which it consists have never been known to form a perfect amalgamation; and at length, in our time, they have been completely and professedly separated. Good histories in the proper sense of the word we have not. But we have good historical romances and good historical essays. The imagination and the reason, if we may use a legal metaphor, have made partition of a province of literature of which they were formerly seized, *per my et per tout*; and now they hold their respective portions in severalty, instead of holding the whole in common. To make the past present, to bring the distant near, to place us in the society of a great man, or on the eminence which overlooks the field of a mighty battle, to invest with the reality of human flesh and blood beings whom we are too much inclined to consider as personified qualities in an allegory, . . . these parts of the duty which properly belongs to the historian have been appropriated by the historical novelist. On the other hand, to extract the philosophy of history, to direct our judgment of events and men, to trace the connection of causes and effects, and to draw from the occurrences of former times general lessons of moral and political wisdom, has become the business of a distinct class of writers.'

Like M. Sismondi, you combine the two functions—that is, you extract the philosophy and direct the judgment, and you likewise attempt to give that lively representation of men, manners, and events which is the part of the historical novelist. The combination, however, does not produce that state of ideal perfection referred to by the essayist. Neither as a writer of history, in the ordinary sense of the word, nor as a writer of fiction, do you stand in the first rank. Your purely historical writings do not, in my estimation, place you among the great historians of our country, nor your fiction among its great novelists. As an historian you have not the reach of Gibbon, nor the brilliancy of Macaulay, nor the exactness of Robertson, nor the acumen and concinnity of Hume, nor the force, the vividness, the lurid picturesqueness of Carlyle ; as a novelist you have not the humour of Cervantes nor the imagination of Scott. But, while saying this, I think that both your scientific studies in history, and your fiction, are distinctly good, notwithstanding all that has been said to the contrary by critics of weight and discernment. *The English in Ireland in the Eighteenth Century* is, to my mind, the very best book on the subject which exists in the English language ; and it should be remembered to your credit that, as a British Tory, you had special temptations to misrepresent our Irish brethren. Those who wish to understand the position of Ireland in the last century cannot do better than read your three volumes. The perusal of them would make clear much that now seems inexplicable, and reasonable much that now seems absurd to superficial observers and politicians who are great in airing ignorance.

Nor in *The Two Chiefs of Dunboy* do I see anything at all unworthy of you. It is not a novel of the very highest order, as I have above hinted, but it is far from being a bad one, or deserving the hard names it has been called in some quarters. One or two sapient critics (conscious, I suppose, of their own superior ability) have pronounced it dull, insipid, and characterless, and one gentleman went so far as to say it positively was not worth reading. I believe some perspicacious person long ago discovered that wholesale condemnation is a comparatively easy thing. It requires no genius to cavil, and a very ordinary talent is equal to the task of pointing out faults. And the worst of it is that even in the best of works there are always faults in plenty to point out. I dare say it would be safe to aver that never in this world has there appeared a work of creative imagination in which defects were not a good deal thicker than plums in a pudding. The greenest critic will show you more defects in a single play of Shakespeare's—say in *Othello*—than your arithmetic can well compute ; and, as to the imperfections of the works of lesser lights, the task of merely enumerating them would be so prodigious and so fearful that the galleys or the treadmill were genuine recreation in comparison. To say, then, that there are blemishes in *The Two Chiefs of Dunboy*, is but to say that it is written by a man and not by an angel or other being of infinite skill and capacity. But with all its faults, I did not find it dull, nor insipid, nor characterless.

It is true that it does not quite succeed in giving that lively representation of men and things of which Macaulay speaks, and which we find at its best in the novels of Scott. Throughout the book there is a lack of freedom; the imagination is for the most part too closely under the control of reason, and only breaks out here and there, as it were, by accident and against your will : in other words, the scientific historian is too much for the creative artist. As Byron said of Campbell, you are afraid to launch out into the deep, to come face to face with the glory and the terror of the storms of emotion ; so that instead of warm and magnificent pictures we have much valuable information about soil and crops, many judicial reflections on political conspiracies, no end of subtle deductions, and a superabundance of extract of philosophy. I have said that you are a man of courage, but in this book you appear as a very timid adventurer, indeed. Courage is no less essential in writing novels than in commanding armies or levying taxes, and the bolder you are the more will be thought of you. Notice how boldly Dumas spreads his wings and looks the sun in the face; notice, too, the audacity of Victor Hugo and Balzac, and, above all, the free and independent movement of Scott. The courage of Scott is sublime. 'Go,' he seems to say to his imagination, 'and where you lead I will follow.' And never once does he falter or look back, never once does he feel dizzy, however high he may be soaring. If you compare one of his historical novels—say *Kenilworth*—with *The Two Chiefs of Dunboy*, you will find the latter superior in every technical detail and inferior in most other qualities that go to the making of a first-rate **novel** or romance—in breadth, in freedom, in warmth of colouring, in picturesqueness, in power of characterisation—in short, in charm and interest. Moreover, there is this difference (and it is one of more consequence than may at first appear) between such a book as *Kenilworth* and *The Two Chiefs of Dunboy*, that while in the former the interest radiates outward from the characters, in the latter it goes inward from what may be called the historical setting. And again Scott blends fact and fancy so cunningly that you cannot distinguish the one from the other, while with you the transition from reality to fiction is often difficult and nearly always clearly perceptible.

But perhaps I am judging you by too high a standard. Every man improves with practice— the genius as well as the dolt, and it may be that enlarged experience would give you confidence enough to throw aside the scientific crutch, and run with the best of them. If it were the work of a young author I should say *The Two Chiefs of Dunboy* is full of promise. The story is occasionally of absorbing interest, and several of the characters are well drawn. Colonel Goring is as fine a fellow as one would wish to meet, loyal and courageous every inch of him, a man with a heart and a conscience and leal to them both; in a word, an Englishman of the very best type—the Puritan type, which has done more for England than all other types combined. One regrets that so good a soldier and so true a man should have fallen in a miserable scuffle in a blacksmith's shop. Morty Sullivan, likewise, is a character that dwells with the reader. The infatuated patriot, burning to free Ireland from the accursed Saxon yoke, willing to sacrifice his life if so be that that will win liberty for his country, is forcibly delineated. He is the best character in the book, and one of the best in recent fiction.   Nor are the minor characters ill-drawn. Sylvester O'Sullivan, Connell, Blake, and Fitzherbert, all reveal themselves in a manner more or less clear and definite. . Then as to incidents, the chase of the *Doutelle* by the Government frigate *Æolus* is capitally described ; so, also, is the duel between Morty Sullivan and Colonel Goring.   And, while enumerating the good points of the book, I must not omit to mention the limpid and delightful flow of its English.   Some hard things have been said of British novelists on the score of style, but he were a hypercritical reader who would find fault with the style of *The Two Chiefs of Dunboy.*

It is not, however, as a novelist, or historian, or essayist, that you are best known, but as a biographer.   For every one who has read your histories, or your essays, or your novel, ten have read your *Life of Thomas* Carlyle.   It is safe to say that no recent biographical work—no recent

work, indeed, of any sort outside of fiction—
has been so widely read or so variously criticised
as that biography of the Sage of Chelsea.

Nor is the reason hard to understand. The
book is one of the most readable biographies
in the language, and the subject is popular, and
peculiar. It was to be expected that of such
an original and unconventional, such an unique
character as Carlyle, there would be extreme
and diverse opinions; and hence there must
likewise be a diversity of view regarding the
manner in which his biographer performed his
task. It was not your fault that so considerable
a section of the reading public came to the
perusal of your work with inveterate prejudices
and manifold preconceptions. But it was a
grave misfortune, for it made it hard—nay, flatly
impossible, to give anything like general satisfaction. Carlyle is a subject that could not be
made universally pleasing. In his lifetime he had
tramped, with no great show of politeness, on a
good many gouty toes, and the owners of the
gouty toes were, of course, savagely on the alert
to avenge their wrongs. Unhappily they had
but too many opportunities. Carlyle had not

the virtue—if virtue it be—of reticence. The
man who could publicly speak of the entire
population of our beloved and enlightened
England as so many millions—mostly fools—
was not likely to be polite in his private utterances.   And assuredly Carlyle was not.   In
conversation as in writing, in diaries as in works
professedly public, he expressed his whole mind
on every subject which occupied his attention,
careless whom he might offend ; adverse and
disagreeable opinions he expressed with the
emphasis of thunder-claps : and when it is
added that his criticisms of contemporaries
were nearly always fiercely hostile or cuttingly
contemptuous, we have a subject that the
highest genius, the genius of Shakespeare himself, could not portray at once truthfully and
pleasingly—at any rate to the majority.   That
your portrait of the Sage is not, in many respects, a flattering one, is at least as much
his fault as yours.   Some of Carlyle's friends
have blamed you for quoting too freely from
his private papers.   They seem to think that if
you had passed over in silence some of the ' ill-
natured criticisms ' of the great critic that the

portrait would be much more agreeable. Doubtless ; but it would not be so near the truth. I
think that if Carlyle himself were to return to
criticise your work he would say that you have
quotéd not too much but too little. I suppose
every biographer worthy of the name must in
some sort be a partisan, but he should yield as
little as possible to all temptations to suppress.
Your hero-worship has led you to suppress a
great deal of what Carlyle wrote, and to this
error of suppression nine-tenths of the blemishes
of the book are directly attributable. As it
stands the picture is more or less distorted, not,
as I believe, because you wished to give an
unfavourable presentation of your subject, but
because of a too great anxiety to conciliate
public opinion. Perfect independence is the
first essential in a biographer of Carlyle. I
believe that if every word ever written by
Carlyle were printed he would be found, what
indeed you often assure us he was, a man
of warm and wide affections, of generous dis-
position, and in the main of liberal judgments. And even in your biography as it
now stands those who study it with open and

free minds will find him anything but malevolent, anything but a backbiter, anything but
an ogre: though those who have suffered
under his lash are likely, despite all the efforts
of a biographer, to continue to regard him as a
monster.

To his great intellectual power you do ample
justice. In your book he stands forth not only
as the most striking personality but as the
greatest writer of later times.

THOMAS HARDY.

To Mr. THOMAS HARDY.

Sir,—I think it would be safe to say that
you are the most distinctively modern of our
living novelists of note.   Mr. Besant may occasionally seem to deal more directly with the
perplexing problems of the day; Mr. Meredith
may appear, to some, to be more emphatically
the intellectual child of the age; but of certain
broad aspects which are as characteristically
nineteenth century as they are characteristically
English, you are, I think, beyond rivalry as a
delineator.   The fashion now obtaining among
the better known of contemporary writers of
fiction is to travel back in search of the
romantic and the picturesque, as if these elements were entirely absent from latter-day life,
instead of being necessarily as perennial as
human nature itself, because they are part of it.
The best work of Mr. Blackmore and Mr.
Stevenson belongs almost exclusively to the

past; even Mr. Besant, notwithstanding his watchful and sympathetic interest in the welfare of the poor, and his sturdy endeavours to be realistic, likes, at times, to disentangle himself from the present, and return to what are gratuitously taken to have been freer and more spacious days. Perhaps there was really more freedom in the world during the rule of darkness than in this era of light; though, if such were the case, the people were singularly blind to their advantages, and grievously given to grumbling; for we do not read the autobiography of any foregoing generation that was satisfied with itself. The habit is always to exaggerate the good things of the past, and depreciate the good things of the present. In retrospection our imaginations are only too apt to 'transfigure dry remainder-biscuit into ambrosia.' 'Ah! beautiful young eyes,' exclaims the poet, 'brimming with love and hope, wholly vanished now in that other world we call the Past, or peering doubtfully through the pensive gloaming of memory, your light impoverishes these cheaper days.' So it ever is. So is it, especially, with the novelist who desires to give

to his work something of that glamour of un-
reality, which is thought by some to be the
final touch of perfection in all things artistic.
A character seen in dim twilight, and supposed
to be sporting a wig, knee-breeches, and silver
buckles, with a sword, which usually proves
more a hindrance than a help, would seem to
be so much more impressive than one encountered in the prosaic glare of the sun, clad
in convenient, if commonplace, clothes, wearing
his natural hair, and unencumbered and unim-
peded by any weapon more unmanageable than
a penknife. So, I say, some novelists would
seem to think. But you are not of the number.
Your work, in texture and spirit, is distinctly of
to-day, an unmistakable product of the last
quarter of the nineteenth century.

But here I would guard against a false im-
plication. The school which is supposed to
represent the culture and taste of the day is
pre-eminently realistic; or, perhaps, more correctly, tediously photographic. It gives the
warts and wrinkles, the angle of the hat and
the cut of the coat, the black eyes and the
abrasions, the bloated countenance, and the

leaky shoes, with great care and fidelity. Nor does it generally fail, with a subtle and refined art peculiar to itself, to give something of the malodorous atmosphere in which its materials mature. But the soul is let as severely alone as if it did not exist. And in truth, for the thorough-going realist, it does not exist. You cannot handle, weigh, and measure it as you would a pound of flesh. It has no solidity; there is nothing tangible and carnal about it; it does not appeal to what some one has called the practical senses, and so it is ignored. Now you are realistic, but you are something more. With an eye for the outward appearance of things as unerring as that of Zola himself, you are kept wholesome and high by that fine idealism which is the distinguishing characteristic of George Sand, and of which every writer, who is not merely a reporter, must have at least a little. Perhaps no living writer can give more genuinely realistic touches than are to be found in abundance in all your books. In the first sentence of *Far from the Madding Crowd*, to take an easy example, when we are told that, ' When Farmer Oak smiled, the corners of his mouth spread till they were within an unimportant distance of his ears, his eyes were reduced to mere chinks, and diverging wrinkles appeared round them, extending upon his countenance like the rays of a rudimentary sketch of the rising sun,' we have a more lively conception of Mr. Oak's facial characteristics than most novelists could give by pages of description. On the other hand, the development of the character is ideal throughout, and Farmer Oak does not turn out the clothes-horse, or spiritual caricature, he would certainly prove in the hands of the realists, whose rigid square-and-rule method of treating life would at times almost lead one to infer that there was no such thing as destiny, and that passion had happily been banished. The Greek conception of Fate was much more pleasant, indeed, much more rational, than the paltry modern doctrines about 'volition.' There is something in the Greek theory which appeals irresistibly to primitive man, if he only had the courage to confess it; the volitional doctrine is a mere feeder and inflater of vanity, and could hardly become popular on any other grounds. Your work has really much of the Greek spirit in it, and is, therefore, unique in the present era. It is realistic, yet distinguished from the productions of the realistic school by a strong element of romance ; it is romantic, yet differs from the writings of the school of pure romance, by an intense and overwhelming reality. This is to say much, because it implies a combination of the best features of the two schools. I do not think the statement that such a combination is seen in your books would be either rash or exaggerated. Your best work does seem to me at once ideal and realistic in the best sense. It deals with present-day life as if there were something perennial in it—that is, that those elements of romance which some profess an nability to discover, save in the remote past, are really as much present now as ever they were —while it does not disdain those apparently prosaic features which the romancists so studiously ignore, but which are so essential to any picture of humanity that has any approximation to completeness.

In my estimation, the great defect of our latter-day fiction is the lack of catholicity and

breadth. Hard and fast lines are drawn between realism and romance, as if in their essence
they were irreconcilably opposed to each other,
instead of being mutually dependent. They
are both in life, and until the world and human
nature change, they are likely to remain in it.
Why, then, should they not go hand in hand in
books? Yet we have two distinct sets of novelists: one loudly declaring that romance is chaff,
and sedulously eschewing it; the other that
realism is mud, and cannot be touched without
contamination. Is it that our writers lack com-
prehensiveness? that their vision is not large
and strong enough to take in the whole scope
of life, as the great ones of past generations
took it in? I can hardly think so. I am of
opinion that perversity and slavish fear of inconsistency are at the bottom of most of the
evils that affect the fiction of to-day. In this
versatile age authors write criticisms as well as
novels. It seems almost compulsory on them
to start with some inelastic theory of life; a
theory that cannot be altered or stretched to
embrace the new conditions of the new times.
And such a theory, once propounded, binds a

critic hand and foot for life, unless he be a person of quite phenomenal honesty and courage. One cannot believe that many of the doctrines one sees upheld by some worthy writers, with so much ingenious sophistry, represent actual beliefs. One can imagine a writer saying to himself something like this: 'I have said so and so on such and such an occasion. I think differently now, but I am committed; there is my past deliverance, and honour is honour. I must be true to myself, I must stick to my word; at all hazards I must be consistent; what I said once I must say now, and to the end of the chapter—heigh-ho.' To be consistent in the eyes of the world, a man must practise in his old age what he has preached in his youth, and at moments when, perhaps, he was not quite sober or responsible. In most cases servile consistency is only dastardly cowardice. Only a few choice souls in each generation have the courage to be nobly inconsistent; and, paradoxical as it may seem, it is precisely this inconsistency that we are in such pressing need of to-day. One is often forced to turn one's back on a friend; why should not a man turn his back on himself when he is conscious of error? We find Scott perpetually disregarding his own dicta; we find Byron doing the same; and it is more than probable that had Shakespeare condescended to give us a systematised theory of life he would have been at variance with himself, ignoring creatively the law he had asserted critically.

You are fortunate in never having hampered yourself with theories. You have laid down no hard and fast rules for yourself, saying 'thus and thus will I do, and thus and thus will I not do.' You take what you want without fear of offending any pet prejudice, or falsifying any blatant oracle, and the consequence is that you draw life as it really exists, with all its sad realism and its fascinating romance. There are some things in *The Mayor of Casterbridge*, for example, to take one instance out of many, so realistic, that even the culture of Boston has signified its approval of them; yet the atmosphere of the book is essentially romantic. Henchard is a romantic character—in some parts his career is pre-eminently romantic; but we follow him through realities which might be paralleled and verified in a hundred towns like Casterbridge, on any day of the week. One thing only disturbs the harmony and general congruity of the book. I refer to Henchard's sale of his wife. That incident, I confess, seems to me to verge rather too closely on the improbable, if not on the farcical or absurd. It would almost appear as if at the outset you had mistaken the scope and quality of your material, and intended the book to be something different from what it is— something half whimsical, perhaps,—and that you only recognised your opportunity when you were well on with your story. The conduct of Henchard's wife, too, is rather—I was going to write disappointing, but surprising would be the better word. I suppose there are women who would tramp round the country, if not quite willingly, at least quite meekly, to be offered for sale at every public-house that is passed, and who would go off quietly with casual sailors as their new lords and masters, but it has never been my fortune to come into contact with them. Considering the frailty and natural curiosity of man, it is, on the whole, just as well that such doves are rare, for one might be tempted to invest—hence domestic complications, and public expense through the necessity of increasing the judicial force in the Divorce Court. But, while taking exception to the sale of the wife, it must be admitted that, in the midst of the incongruity, there is a reality that reminds one of Henry Fielding, or, perhaps more forcibly, of Jonathan Swift, and almost convinces one that it is right and proper for men to dispose of wives who prove an encumbrance, and altogether natural that wives should be obedient and submissive in such transactions. In *Gulliver*, once get over the absurdity of the Flying Island, and all seems as natural as need be; in like manner, when one is past the sale of the wife in *The Mayor of Casterbridge* there is nothing in it to disturb credulity. In other respects the book is, like all your books, masterly. Michael Henchard is a splendid character—one of the best you have ever drawn. Even in his degradation he is noble. He is a creature of impulses, but of generous impulses, so that often when he is doing that for which the law would punish him, the reader's sympathies are entirely with him. Had he been less magnanimous one feels that he would have been more successful (not as an artistic creation, but as a man of business), but the interest would not then be half so keen. His treatment of Donald Farfrae is almost heroic. Not the loss of his business, not the blasting of his dearest ambitions, not insults and aggravations could make Henchard anything else than generous. Even when he and Farfrae have quarrelled out-right, and have met to dispose of each other for ever, Henchard's better nature does not sink out of sight.

In the fight between the two men, for instance, Henchard begins with the intention of killing Farfrae—and he could have done it, there is no doubt about that—and he ends by handing him his life and reproaching himself for his disgrace-ful behaviour.

Farfrae is hardly so good a creation. He is more conventional, more bookish, the result of reading rather than observation and inspiration. You do not know the Scotsman as well as you know the rural Englishman. Even Donald's speeches are rather strange to one who knows much of the country and people lying beyond

the Tweed. One might, for instance, inquire
what Presbyterian cream is, and how it could
be as *warreming* to the stomach as Casterbridge
ale ? and a summer *jarreny* to Edinboro', would,
doubtless, be a very pleasant novelty. But even
Farfrae is conceivable and companionable.

Indeed, I think it would be quite impossible
for you to touch a character, however lightly,
without imparting to it something of the vitality
which genius alone can give. Let there be no
mincing of words. It may be a heresy, after
all that has been said and written, to assert that
such a thing as genius exists at all, and that you
are as great a master of character as any novelist
whom this country has produced, scarcely excepting even Scott, or Fielding, or Thackeray—
it may be a heresy, I say, to state as much ; but
then one must be heretical occasionally, in order
to be truthful. All your books that I have ever
read are 'masterly in minute characterisation
and delicious in humour.' I have spoken at
some length of Henchard, and called him one
of your best creations, but he is not, by a long
way, your only good one. Gabriel Oak, and a
score or two others, might be named in the

same sentence.   And for general excellence it seems to me that you are almost, if not quite, unmatched among contemporary novelists. Such a book as *The Woodlanders* is enough to make one feel proud of one's generation, and, while it is always hard to predict what will live and what will not, I think it might surely be prophesied that that book will be known long after your generation.   So, also, one would be inclined to say, will *Far from the Madding Crowd*, though not without a touch of melo-drama here and there that is hardly in your best style ; while, if fidelity and idealism count for anything, *Under the Greenwood Tree* is as sure of life as anything that has been done in our day.

I understand you are no favourite with the young lady who patronises the circulating lib-raries.   She is in the habit of making mar-ginal notes in your books which are sometimes more entertaining than complimentary. Precisely why the fair one quarrels with you is, of course, among the mysteries of the world, but it is vaguely understood she considers herself slan-dered in your female characters, so she calls you 'that horrid man Hardy,' a description which I suppose, to the feminine mind, expresses the height of disgust. What would she have? Mr. Lang, in upholding Thackeray in the face of detraction on the score of his female characters, says that people should really find fault with nature, and not with the novelist who copies nature. You might make a similar reply to your feminine critics. So long as Bathshebas are tolerably common in life, why should they not have their portraits painted? Your women are not conventional. They are not of the flaccid, pink and white type; but neither, so far as I can remember, are they inherently wicked. Let us have living creations—that is the great want in fiction—and that you give us in your women as well as in your men. Let us be thankful.

For power in describing scenery and natural objects generally, I hardly know your superior among novelists since Scott. Nay, I think that, in some respects, you are above the master himself. If he had the freer hand, you have, perhaps, the truer. Everywhere you are just as poetic as he, and generally far more minute—

without being in the least tedious.   There are
as choice bits of description in your books as
are to be met with in all fiction—I had almost
said in all literature.   In reading you, one often
witnesses a whole world bursting into bloom;
we feel the fragrance in our nostrils, and all but
see the circulation of the sap in those woods
you so much delight to describe.   We have
writers who are more fastidious about having
nature always in holiday attire, but none who
paints her more truthfully or feelingly as she
is ordinarily, nor is there anything in the least
sentimental in your love of nature.   Rousseau
has not infected you with his weakness, and
you have not copied the lackadaisical whin-
ings of so many of his disciples.   In a word, in
describing nature, as in all else you do, you are
strong, and not only strong, but delightful.

JOHN GREENLEAF WHITTIER.

To Mr. JOHN GREENLEAF WHITTIER.

Sir,—In many respects yours has been an ideal life. By this I do not mean that you have enjoyed immunity from the cares and crosses, the heart-break and the strife, that, in the main, are the portion of mankind ; that you have passed your days in a bower of roses, trilling daintily like a species of mocking-bird, as the humour seized you, or in a library jingling euphonious rhymes designed for the delectation of the sensuous ear. Quite the contrary. Nor do you altogether realise to one's imagination that majestic picture of Milton's of a 'poet soaring in the high regions of his fancy, with his garland and singing robes about him.' You have, indeed, soared in the high regions of fancy, else had you never earned the honourable title of poet ; but for garland you have had the smoke of battle on your brow, and your singing robe has been a common jacket. Your life has not been one of Sybaritic ease and ample leisure, but of hot and arduous conflict. Nevertheless I repeat that in many respects it has been an ideal one, for your efforts have mightily hastened a glorious march from darkness into light, from mephitic pestilential swamps, suffocating in their noisomeness, to breezy, healthy heights, where the soul of manhood can expand and breathe as becomes it. In the pride of your young strength you girded the sword on the thigh, and went fearlessly forth to fight the powers of tyranny and oppression, with hardly any support, save that sublime conviction which has so often won the day in unequal struggles —the conviction that, ultimately, wrong must perish and right must triumph. The battle was fierce and obstinate, for the enemy was strong, and long was the issue dubious, but in the darkest hour you never faltered. With a faith as unflinching as that of our own brave Cromwell, you, and the noble ones banded with you, held on, growing ever the more determined the heavier the odds against you. When Church and State opposed you, when Cabinet Ministers denounced you as revolutionary and anarchic, and ministers of religion strove to prove from the Bible that the white man had a vested right to traffic in human flesh, you defiantly and scornfully asked regarding the free citizen—

> ' Must he be told his freedom stands
>   On slavery's dark foundations strong—
> On breaking hearts and fettered hands,
>   On robbery and crime and wrong ?
> That all his fathers taught is vain—
> That freedom's emblem is the chain?'

Then the moneyed opposition, stung into defiant rage, after prophesying failure, asked what were you that you should presume to disturb the economy of nature; that you should dictate to your superiors, the holders of human property, whose rights were perhaps equal to those of the Deity Himself? You were unknown, you were obscure, you were without influence, all of which was true; but you were not without zeal, and so you fought on, never despairing, till at last the head of the hydra was crushed, and in view of the concourse of evil prophets, many of them, I regret to say, hailing from our own free isle, you sheathed the sword and put on the victor's crown. It was a glorious triumph ; and now in the serenity of old age, with the consciousness of duty well done, you are reaping your reward in a fame as wide as the civilised world, and the lasting affection of all lovers of liberty. It is a sweet and peaceful evening after a stormy day. You could not yourself have desired a serener or a more victorious close to the battle. Those who were once most virulent in their abuse, and most confident in their predictions of failure, are now amongst your most enthusiastic eulogists. No voice now dares to defend the monstrous wrong at which you hurled your thunders more than a generation ago. Slavery has been stamped out of existence among the Anglo-Saxon race, and on the bright roll of the vanquishers there is no name that will prove more enduring than that of John Greenleaf Whittier.

Edmund Burke said, in passing a panegyric on Fox for so valiantly espousing the cause of the people of India, that 'it was not only in the Roman customs, but it is in the nature and constitution of things that calumny and abuse are essential parts of triumph.' For you the calumny and abuse are past, buried with the hatred which gave them birth, and only the splendid victory and the memory of your own heroic conduct remain. Burke and Fox, and those associated with them in their high endeavour, did not succeed in all their noble aims regarding the people of India. They did not, nobly as they struggled, even 'secure to every man the rice in his pot'; but you and those who worked with you made a free man of every slave within the bounds and dominions of the United States.

I am well aware that in the popular mind you are not much associated with those reforms in the laws of your country which made so many millions of bondmen free. We talk of William Lloyd Garrison, and Wendell Phillips, and Abraham Lincoln, but we too often forget the claims of J. G. Whittier. Not that you would yourself put forward any claims or feel disappointed at being passed over in commemoration odes and orations; but if, as the old proverb holds, justice is a jewel, then each should have his right reward. We honour the names and memories of Garrison, Phillips, and Lincoln.

Garrison was undoubtedly the protagonist in the great drama. The young man in the little back office, in the little back street of Boston, who wrote and printed his obscure sheet himself, deserves the highest encomiums that tongue or pen can pass on him. He was the first to inaugurate a systematic campaign against slavery, and was, moreover, I believe, the means of enlisting your sympathies and services in the cause of emancipation; so that in connection with the abolition movement his claims to honour are paramount. Nor will the powerful aid of Wendell Phillips—the silvery-tongued, as his compatriots loved to call him—the greatest orator of the century, as he has been styled by so good a judge as your friend, the late John Bright,—his aid, I say, will not readily be forgotten by the friends of freedom. And surely the world will long cherish a kindly feeling for the memory of Abraham Lincoln. Old Abe— the homely, the genial, the shrewd, the foreseeing, the great, who was equally at home whether entertaining the loafers about a country grocery store with yarns, or directing the affairs of a State; the provincial attorney who piloted a nation through the most gigantic conflict that ever taxed the manhood and energy of a people, the 'new birth of our new soil, our first American,' as Mr. Lowell has described him. Surely the world will never forget him. For hardly in modern times has such a ruler, so sagacious, so far-seeing, so patient, so courageous, so hopeful, and so helpful, either risen from the ranks of the people or stepped from the purple.

But his work, and the work of the others I have named, being purely political, is easily seen and easily appraised, whereas the value of your work is hard to reckon. When poetry is an element in the work of reformation, it is almost certain to remain unappreciated. The poet works silently and mysteriously in the deep places of the soul, and so ignorant and careless are people that the impulse which he gives is often ascribed to somebody or something else. Poetry is vaguely acknowledged to have an ennobling influence, but it is not thought to have much potency as a political factor. Yet, Mr. Lowell claims for it 'an influence more durable and more widely operative than that exerted by any other form in which human genius has found expression.' And beyond question he is right. The influence of poetry in any cause it espouses is absolutely incalculable. When Fletcher of Saltoun said, 'Give me the making of a nation's songs, and I care not who makes its laws,' he was not overrating the power of poetry, as might very easily be proved. It has been said that the poems of Homer did more than aught else to unite the Grecian States. We see the influence of song in the struggles of Scotland and Ireland. Ritson assures us that the poetic squibs of the Cavaliers, during the Commonwealth, kept alive the spirit of loyalty, and ultimately contributed to the Restoration ; and so I might go on giving endless instances of the power of song over a people's hearts and minds. But why multiply examples with your own case before us ? It is a fact which scarcely requires assertion, that your poetry proved a mighty help to those who were labouring to free the African in America. You, perhaps, more than any other, with the single exception of Garrison, prepared the way for that act of manumission which has made the memory of Abraham Lincoln as lasting as the human race itself.

A poet, however, cannot be an active and conscious reformer with impunity. Much of your poetry having been written for a specific purpose, to serve a passing, if pressing, need, has already lost much of its value as literature. A recent and sympathetic critic has well said, ' Mr. Whittier can afford to own that he has sometimes failed to rise above the level of the verse maker. A writer who celebrates the events of the passing hour must expect the lustre of some performances to fade with the interests which called them forth, and in the mass of Mr. Whittier's productions, representing as it does the fruitage of a long and busy life, there is much, undoubtedly, of an ephemeral character ; but there is an abundance of durable work of a peculiar and rare quality, and there are certain themes which, by right of discovery, this writer has made his own.' Yes, there is much that is durable after the patriotic and indignant outbursts of verse have been excised ; much that might make that strong address of Mr. Swinburne's as appropriate to you as to your compatriot and brother poet, Walt Whitman :—

> ' O strong-winged soul with prophetic
>   Lips, hot with 'the blood-beats of song,
> With tremor of heart-strings magnetic,
>   With thoughts as thunders in throng,
> With consonant ardours of chords
> That pierce men's souls as with swords,
>   And hale them hearing along ! '

If you could not in comparison to the mighty ones of the realm of song be called great, if

> ' Not yours the song whose thunderous chime
>   Eternal echoes render ;
> The mournful Tuscan's haunted rhyme,
>   And Milton's starry splendour,'

it is certainly a song which sweetens toil. Of you it might be said what you have yourself so feelingly sung of Burns—

> ' Through all his tuneful art how strong
>   The human feeling gushes!
> The very moonlight of his song
>   Is warm with smiles and blushes.'

But though you invite comparison with Burns, I do not mean to imply that you are his equal in poetic power. You have lyric force, but you have not *his* lyric force. You have insight, but not *his* insight ; you have tenderness and passion, but they are not *his* tenderness and passion. Of his powers of caricature and satire you have very little, and of his humour less. Burns has sung the loves and lives of men and women as they never were sung before his time, as they have not been sung since, and as, in all probability, they never will be sung again. Your work then has not the high poetic qualities of Burns's, and that to be sure is no disparagement to you, seeing that Burns is out and away the greatest poet we have had since the days of Milton. But you resemble him in many ways, and follow at a distance where he leads. Like him you sing of humble things; like him you take for your text that

> ' Rank is but the guinea stamp,
>   The man's the gowd for a' that,'

only your sermon, as compared with his, is pitched in a minor key.

Nor in another line which is fashionable just now, and for which you have shown a fondness, do you compare quite favourably with some of the older writers—I mean the ballad. Charming and pathetic ballads you have indeed given us, as any one who has read ' Mary Garvin ' and

‘ Maud Muller ’ knows,—ballads that are among the best of their class produced in the present century. But this century hardly excels in ballad writing. Nothing that you have done, nothing that any of your fellow-poets of recent times have done, will stand comparison, say with ‘ The Twa Corbies ’ or ‘ Fair Helen of Kirkconnell.’ What a vista these simple words open to the imagination !—

> ‘ There were three rauens sat on a tre,
> They were as blacke as they might be ;
> The one of them said to his mate,
> “ Where shall we our breakfast take ? ”
> “ Downe in yonder greene field
> There lies a knight slain under his shield.” ’

No more is wanted ; the imagination fills up all the rest, and one sees the ghastly banquet spread with a vividness that is positively painful. And what modern verse so well expresses agony of soul as these fearful and tragic lines :—

> ‘ Curst be the heart that thought the thought,
> And curst the hand that fired the shot,
> When in my arms burd Helen dropped
> And died to succour me ! ’

There is the force of incipient madness there, the heart-strings are cracking, the whole being is thrilled with the ecstasy of despair, and the grim spectre is waiting for his prey in the background. We cannot produce such effects now by the use of written words, probably because we have lost our simplicity and cannot feel with sufficient intensity. Perhaps those old ballads are after all too intense; perhaps their lightning-like brevity strikes home too quickly to be altogether comfortable. We like to take our pleasures quietly—at any rate such pleasures as we derive from reading poetry: and the man who stirs us too strongly is quite as likely to get a reprimand as a nod of thanks or a smile of encouragement. Your ballads, and indeed all your poems, give satisfaction without rousing to any painful pitch of excitement. And they are as pure and fresh and wholesome as the breezes blowing among the pines of your own Bay State, or the springs gushing from its hillsides. If your poetry cannot in strictness be called great, it is at least genuine, and that is no slight thing at a time when verbal flippancies and oddities of form are so often the care of our poets. You are a true child of nature—unspoiled by any affectation. What you write

I

comes from the heart and goes to the heart. You are no mere jingler of rhyme; there is an earnest aim in all your work; and it has merit enough, I believe, to hand your name down to future generations.

But I should imagine that you are comparatively careless of fame. After all, there is but one thing that can give solid comfort in the sunset hour of life, and that is the consciousness of having used one's talents in the highest service to which it was possible to put them. That consciousness is surely yours. You have done what you could for your fellow-men; you have fought the battle of the weak, and helped to raise the down-trodden and the oppressed. There is a glory higher than the laurel of the poet: the glory of good deeds done in behalf of suffering humanity; and it is yours. You are a poet, a true and sweet one, and something better.

ALGERNON CHARLES SWINBURNE.

To Mr. ALGERNON CHARLES SWINBURNE.

Sir,—It is strictly within the limits of truth to say that you are one of the hardest literary enigmas of the age. To guess what your guiding principle in public is—supposing such a thing to be among your personal possessions—would require not merely human ingenuity and penetration, but something of that high gift of clairvoyance or second-sight which is thought to be the peculiar attribute of witches and beings of a superhuman order of intelligence. In the public—and the public surely includes the literary—conduct of most men and women, there is some leading principle, by the aid of which one may arrive at some sort of judgment concerning the motive of their lives. In yours there should seem to be nothing of the kind. Your career, so far as I have ever been able to discover, is safely above the charge of congruity, consistency, or unity.   It is your forte to be for ever disappointing.   If one seize on what appears to be a trait, in the fond imagination that at last he has found a clew which will guide him in the labyrinth of conflicting evidence, he is apt to find it negatived at some important turn, and come back on his hands like a dishonoured cheque.   Nor are what in the writings of others would be accepted as pledges to be depended on.   *Fronti nulla fides.*   You have the most daring, the most fascinating, the most tantalising way of contradicting yourself. You are consistent only in your inconsistency. You would appear to treat each separate thought and opinion, to which you give utterance, as if they had no connection with past thoughts and opinions, and were to have no connection with those which were to come.   Alike as a poet, a politician, and a critic, you have 'gone back on yourself,' as the Americans say, regardless, contemptuously regardless, of uniformity and the opinion of the world.   What you said yesterday, with the solemnity and assurance of an oracle, is flatly contradicted by what you say to-day; and it may, without misgiving, be assumed that what you say to-day will be contradicted by the judgment on men and things it may please you to pass to-morrow. You are heroically true to yourself in this, that no past utterance of yours can be relied on as giving the faintest indication of your future utterances.

This, be it frankly admitted, implies no ordinary degree of courage. The fear of inconsistency is, on the authority of the old adage, the fear of fools. And to be sure we all live to learn. It is beyond all question better to discard the opinions of the past, if we discover them to be wrong, than to stick to them at the expense of truth, and for the mere sake of making a creditable appearance in the eyes of men. But there are two sorts of inconsistency: that which springs from deep sincerity, and that which springs from sheer capriciousness. In other words, there is the inconsistency of advancing reason and intelligence, and the inconsistency of perverse humours. I am not going to say, nor to imply, which of the two is yours. I might make a guess and be wrong, in which case I should be doing you an injustice. Like

a certain astute politician, of whom you have
doubtless read—

> ' I don't make no insinooations ;
> **I jest let on I smell a rat.'**

Old-fashioned science taught us that our
substance changed once in every seven years ;
new-fashioned science, by one of its brightest
apostles, Dr. Holmes, tells us that, instead of
undergoing a change every seven years, our
bodies really change with every breath we draw.
Perhaps it is with the mental as with the material part of us ; so that it may be every minute
witnesses several complete changes in the constitution of the mind. Bailey, indeed, says
distinctly that ' man's mind is like the moon,'
and the moon, we know, is subject to change.
And your own case might be instanced as an
argument in favour of the theory. I am not
jesting, but going strictly and seriously on the
evidence furnished by your own published
works. If we are to attach any importance to
an author's dogmatic expression of opinion, you
certainly are addicted to change. You began
your career as a red-hot Republican ; to-day
you are a Tory of the Tories, as rank and

haughty, and scornful as the best, or worst, of those whose special function in life it is to trample on the liberties of the people. In the ardour of your youth, and the first full force of your manhood, you sympathised nobly and eloquently with every aspiration for freedom, wherever such was to be detected. You were with Poland and Hungary in their struggles to throw off the yoke of a grinding and alien power; you were with France in her efforts to bring the tenure of Courts to a close. No living author has wasted so much frenzied rhetoric in espousing the cause of the masses against the classes. Yet, that there might be nothing wanting in the incongruity and inconsistency of your public appearance, no sooner does there come an appeal to your own door than you hasten with more than aristocratic rigour and haughtiness to stop the ear that you may not hear, and harden the heart that you may not understand; nay, you, who might not seem to have had any special call that way, turn aside to tell an oppressed people that liberty— the liberty which Englishmen are never tired of boasting about—is not among the things to which they have any right.

In purely literary matters, likewise, we find
the same charming inconstancy to self distinguishing your career at nearly every point.
We find you raising an idol to-day, for no
better reason, as it should seem, than that you
might have the pleasure of demolishing it to-
morrow. Lest I might be accused of unfairness and exaggeration by those who have not
had the pleasure of witnessing your almost in-
credible agility in changing front and colour,
let me quote one or two of your judgments side
by side. At one time we discover you praising
Byron, and pouring out your indignation upon
all who dare say a word against him. ' The
excellence of sincerity and strength,' you say,
' without these no poet can live ; but few have
ever had so much of them as Byron.' As the
natural corollary to that take the following :—
' He ' (Byron) ' can only claim to be acknowledged ·as a poet of the third class, who now
and then rises into the second, but speedily
relapses into the lower element where he was
born. . . . How very bad it ' (his lordship's unfortunate poetry) ' was ; how very hollow were
its claims ; how very ignorant, impudent, and

foolish was the rabble rout of its adorers. . . .
In all the composition of his highly composite
nature there was neither a note of real music
nor a gleam of real imagination.' Truly there
is no craven fear of inconsistency to be discovered there.

Again, look on these two pictures : 'His
glorious courage, his excellent contempt for
things contemptible, and hatred of hateful men,
are enough of themselves to embalm and endear
his memory in the eyes of all who are worthy to
pass judgment on him.'

'The malevolent and cowardly conceit of a
Byron, ever shuffling and swaggering, and cring-
ing, and back-biting in a breath.' Once more
look at the noble partisanship that flies to arms
whenever the name or fame of the revered one
is menaced. 'At the first chance given or
taken, every obscure and obscene thing that
lurks for pay or prey among the fouler shallows
and thickets of literature flew against him ;
every hound and every hireling lavished upon
him the loathsome tribute of their abuse ; all
nameless creatures that nibble and prowl, upon
whom the serpent curse has fallen to go upon

his belly and eat dust all the days of his life, assailed him with their foulest venom and their keenest fangs.'

Later on there was nothing discoverable in Bryon but 'grandiose meanness,' and 'faithless-ness.' Clearer judgment said that he had no honour, that he was a sneak, had no great regard for the truth, and, in a general way, was no gentlemen.

Unhappy Byron ! To be kissed and caressed, extolled, defended, and then cast into the gutter and trampled on, is not a desirable fate. And, what are we to say of him who does the kissing, and the caressing, and the extolling, and the trampling ? At one time the noble qualities of Byron were enough 'to embalm and endear his memory in the eyes of all who are worthy to pass judgment on him,' but now—now alas ! all that is changed. Or, is it that Mr. Algernon Charles Swinburne is no longer worthy to pass judgment on him ? The moralist assures us that man changes.

At one time you spoke respectfully of the ' great character ' of Carlyle, but lest you should be suspected of remaining too long of one mind you have since denounced the 'great character' in such Billingsgate as certainly is no credit to the literature of the day. Nor are these the only cases in which you exhibit your fascinating variableness.

To take just one more instance out of many. There was a time when you sent a fervent message of admiration and esteem to the venerable poet of America—Walt Whitman—in this strain :—

> ' Send but a song over sea for us,
>   Heart of their hearts who are free.
>   Heart of their singer, to be for us
>   More than our singing can be ;
>   Ours, in the tempest at error,
>   With no light but the twilight of terror,
>   Send us a song over the sea.'

But now Walt Whitman is a clod-hopper, with as little music and as little imagination as the charlatan and impostor Byron. In one of your critical pieces you say, 'Sir Walter Scott was neither a profound nor a pretentious critic, neither a refined nor an eccentric theorist, but his judgments have always the now more than ever invaluable qualities of clearness and consistency.' What a double-edged sword criticism is, to be sure! I wonder if any writer coming after us will have courage enough to say that the writings of Algernon Charles Swinburne have the invaluable quality of consistency. I wonder, also, if any subsequent critic can find it in his heart to attribute humility to them. ''There is small chance of truth at the goal,' says Coleridge, 'where there has not been a childlike humility at the starting-post.' Neither at start, nor at finish, do you ever seem to me to be oppressed by any humility.

And yet, let me candidly confess, that to my mind you have given us some of the very best criticism which has directed the taste of this generation. Those very qualities which under the influence of prejudice make you so perverse and so misleading, make you, when free from prepossession, a valuable and companionable critic. To the first-rate critic three things are essential, perspicacity, sympathy, and independence. The last you invariably have, the two former you have when you are at your best; as, for instance, in your *Study of Shake-speare*, and your *Study of Victor Hugo*, and your various criticisms on Shelley. I question if there is in the language a better 'Study' of Shakespeare than yours. It is sympathetic; it glows with noble appreciation; it is luminous and just; in some parts really creative, and it always transcends the commonplace. The best way to understand Shakespeare is, of course, to read him, but those who wish to get at his best points by the short and easy byway of criticism cannot do better than take you for their guide. And, indeed, inasmuch as Shakespeare is often obscure in his greatness, the most intelligent readers might profit by a perusal of your book. I do not say that you light up the whole of Shakespeare—that perhaps were impossible save to an intellect as great as his own—but you do illumine in many dark places, and even where such is not the case, your writing is valuable and interesting simply as a piece of literature.

Your *Hugo*, also, is a masterly performance—masterly in its grasp, its liberality, its contempt for conventionalities, its force, its sweep and splendour of diction. In it, better than in any recent criticisms which I can at the moment of writing think of, one sees how happily and

beneficially the understanding and imagination
can work together. It would be hard, I think,
to give a more compendious estimate of Victor
Hugo and his work in a single sentence than
the following :—'In the first poem' (the 'Con-
templations') 'a sublime humility finds such
expression as should make manifest to the
dullest eye, not clouded by malevolence and
insolent conceit, that when this greatest of
modern poets asserts in his own person the
high prerogative, and assumes for his own spirit
the high office of humanity to confront the
darkest problem, and to challenge the utmost
force of intangible and invisible justice as of
visible and tangible iniquity ; of all imaginable
as of all actual evil ; of superhuman indifference
as well as of human wrongdoing ; it is no
merely personal claim that he puts forward, no
vain egotistic arrogance that he displays ; but
the right of a reasonable conscience, and the
duty of a righteous faith, common to all men
alike, in whom intelligence of right and wrong,
perception of duty or conception of conscience,
can be said to exist at all.'

The book abounds in high and noble passages—passages that lift one away out of the common atmosphere altogether, and reveal other worlds than we are accustomed to look upon.

It is written of course in a spirit of frank admiration, almost idolatry. There are many expressions throughout it that one's calmer judgment might be inclined to tone down; many epithets that the critical mind, in its normal icy condition, might be disposed to consider hyperbolical; but the judicious reader will overlook all that and think only of the noble admiration of one poet for another, and the eloquence that dazzles and enchants. Your *Victor Hugo* is, with the possible exception of your *Shakespeare*, if even it can be made an exception, your best work in prose. It is a work which almost deserves to live beside the works of even

> ' That one whose name gives glory,
> One man whose life makes light,
> One crowned and throned in story
> Above all empires' height.'

Your work as a poet still remains to be considered. In it, as in so much of your prose, you are an unequal, an erratic, and tantalising craftsman, much given to paradox and often not a little mysterious. Your poetry is hard to test by any accepted standard, for you are a man of new departures. You cannot be considered a useful poet, as Mr. Birrell once designated your opponent in so many fights, the late Matthew Arnold. I am not quite sure, indeed, what the author of *Obiter Dicta* meant by the word useful. Either my memory is treacherous, or he was not particularly explicit on the point. He could not, I should think, have meant that a poet ought to enter into competition with stockbrokers, and advise us, in versified circulars, as to the best and readiest means of making money. That could hardly have been his meaning. Nor could he have meant that our singers ought to give hints on household management. I have no doubt whatever that recipes in verse, and axioms of domestic economy in rhyme, would be highly interesting, though, I dare say, the cook would prefer her instructions, and the housewife her hints, in plain prose. The exigencies of rhyme are so great that mistakes would almost certainly be made if the poet were to invade the kitchen. Therefore Mr. Birrell could not have meant *that*. Nor could he have meant that it is the poet's duty to consider whether or not the working-man ought to buy his provisions in co-operative stores. All that, I should imagine, is outside the sphere of the singer. Of course poets can be useful in a way. They are known to be authorities on all erotic questions, so that they might fairly be expected to help an awkward and bashful bachelor in the choice of a wife. But so far as things practical are concerned, this is about all that a poet in his poetical capacity could do. To be sure there are higher and less direct ways of being useful; but in these I do not think that your work is of any appreciable value. I do not think any one would go to you for solace in the hour of trouble, or for encouragement in the hour of doubt and despair. What, then, are your claims as a poet? Perhaps your own answer is the best that could be given. 'The test of the highest poetry,' you say in one of your essays, 'is that it eludes all tests. Poetry in which there is no element at once perceptible and indefinable by any reader or hearer of poetic instinct may have every other good quality, but it is not poetry—above

all, it is not lyric poetry—of the first water.
There must be something in the mere progress
and resonance of the words, some secret in the
very motion and cadence of the lines, inexplicable by the most sympathetic acuteness of
criticism.   Analysis may be able to explain how
the colours of this flower of poetry are created
and combined, but never of what process its
odour is produced.'   Excellently put, and true,
too, in a sense.   But you know extremes meet.
If the highest poetry is indefinable, so, also, is
the lowest.   Genius and insanity, philosophers
tell us, walk hand in hand, and their utterances
are sometimes hard to distinguish ; so that while
it may be perfectly true that the highest poetry
is indefinable, such a test does not always suffice
to show us what really is poetry, and what is not.
Mr. Robert Montgomery was considered a great
poet until Macaulay took him in hand ; and his
poetry certainly was indefinable.   I am not sure,
however, that its flowers had any odour, unless,
being rooted in the nether regions, they smelled
of brimstone ; so that might have been a guide
in estimating their value.   Apart, however, from
all whimsical speculations, if we are to test you

by your own standard you certainly are a poet. Your poetry, as I have said, does not comfort nor give heart, differing in that respect from the poetry of the world's greatest sons of song ; but much of it is perfectly indefinable, in the best sense of that word. Like Shelley's and Coleridge's it depends a great deal on 'the mere progress and resonance of the words.' It is not stimulating poetry that is so dependent. It is not the poetry of Shakespeare, nor the poetry of Dante, nor even the poetry of Wordsworth. But, in your case, it is poetry all the same. As a specimen let us take the following from 'The Garden of Cymodoce'—

 'O flower of all wind flowers and sea flowers,
  Made lovelier by love of the sea
 Than thy golden own field flowers or tree flowers
  Like foam of the sea-facing tree !
 No foot but the sea-mew's there settles
  On the spikes of thine anther-like horns,
 With snow-coloured spray for thy petals,
  Black rocks for the thorns.'

There is not much there to lay hold on, yet one feels instinctively that it is poetry ; and most of your 'thunderous verse' is as light and intangible. As a dramatist I cannot notice your work further than to say, that in parts of your dramas you seem to be at your best ; and that here and there, particularly in *Mary Stuart* and *Atalanta in Calydon*, you show a high and rare power, and a grasp of character, for which such poems as 'Songs before Sunrise' would not prepare one.

HALL CAINE.

To Mr. HALL CAINE.

Sir,—If I were to make a prediction as to which of the younger novelists of England should ultimately take the lead — should, to quote Mr. Buchanan, ' rise in the end to genuine eminence, to the sad sunless aureole of fame,' I think I should name you. To many I dare say my choice would appear singular, for there are some of your younger contemporaries in the field of fiction who have been received with fourfold the acclaim ever accorded to you. Yet, in spite of this discouraging fact, there is not one among those who are still on the upward grade whose work seems to me at once so excellent a thing as it stands, and so splendid an earnest of what is to come. *The Deemster*, for example, besides being a fine piece of work in itself, full of power and vital human interest, is perhaps the most magnificent pledge of coming achievement in the realm of imaginative prose that has been given to the English people for at least a decade. Indeed, it is a book so rich in promise· that one might not unreasonably regard its writer as the possible successor of Scott. Certainly in it he has what Mr. Lowell calls ' the large stride of the elder race.' The book belongs to the big, the broad, the strong and impressive order of fiction. It has a spaciousness of air, an unconventionality, and a reach of imagination which make it rare among recent novels. Apart from the prospect which it holds out, if I were to call it one of the best things done by any living English novelist I might be accused of exaggeration, yet I think the statement would be tolerably near the truth. Some of Mr. Hardy's novels, and at least one of Mr. Blackmore's, surpass it, in my estimation, in the requirements of high art as well perhaps as in general power, but that, I think, can be said of no work but theirs. In saying this, I do not forget the claims of Mr. Meredith, whose wit and penetration are unequalled among latter-day writers of fiction, if not indeed among writers of fiction of any day. Moreover, I suspect that he excels you in single scenes. In these he is sometimes unmatchable. Some parts of *The Egoist* are almost Shakespearian in their impressiveness, and are assuredly among the strongest in the entire range of British fiction ; yet I think that as an organic whole, *The Egoist* hardly equals *The Deemster* ; and I should be disposed to say that if Sir Willoughby Patterne is one of the characters of the century, Daniel Mylrea is another. There is, of course, no resemblance between the two characters ; nor are your literary methods the least like those of Mr. Meredith. He is finical and elaborate, an artist in phrase, a wit taking the keenest delight in sparkling and pungent witticisms, and prepared at any moment to sacrifice the heart for the head. You, on the other hand, are comparatively indifferent to literary decoration, and pay more heed to the emotions than to the intellect. Elaborate, in a literary sense, you certainly are not, nor do you pay any assiduous court to the Comic Muse. You have apparently no time to coin epigrams ; if you have humour you never jest ; satire you indulge in sparely, and your moral reflections are rather hammer-strokes than sermons. Dante himself is not more economical of words.   In *The Deemster* the effects are rendered with almost unexampled rapidity.   The imagination seems all aglow, and will not be checked in pouring out its shapes.   Indeed, if one were inclined to cavil at anything in the book, one would say that the pace is too impetuous, that the artist, eager to catch his own conceptions in their virgin force and freshness, dashed them on canvas, with little regard to finish or technical detail.   This, I take it, is because you approach your subject from the human instead of the literary side.   Such is not the method in fashion now, but it is the method of all the masters, from Cervantes and Scott down. Humanity first, literary embellishments afterwards.   With you the latter receive perhaps too scant attention ; and, as a consequence, your work, compared with that of some of your contemporaries, has an occasional aspect of bluntness.   But, on the other hand, no exercise of technical skill, no verbal ornamentation, could add one whit to the vividness of the pictures presented.   One forgets the abruptness of style in the absorbing interest of the story, and the fierce masterfulness of the characters; for they have a primitive strength that is overwhelming.

One hears, indeed, enough, and more than enough, about style; and is glad to have it sometimes thrust into the background; to feel that the life of a book lies in the matter, not in the manner, and that forceful thought is never without fit expression. We are all stylists in this age. We can play tricks with words that would astonish our ancestors, could they hear them, as I dare say they will astonish posterity. From M. Daudet to Mr. Stevenson and Mr. Howells, the cry is so much for style, that one is often reminded of Richter's gibe, that want of matter makes one think too much of language. The inordinate and irrational stress which is at present laid on style in some quarters makes it with many not a means, but an end. It is as if the mathematician thought only of his instruments, or the chemist of his crucible. Mr. James, for instance, is so clever a stylist that in those curious books which he designates novels he can altogether dispense with humanity and its sorry traits and passions, and with plot and its ridiculous evolutions, and entertain the reader with neat phrases, and elegant and elaborate paragraphs about nothing. A wonderful achievement, betokening great ingenuity ; but surely literature ought to be something more than a species of legerdemain. Do not suppose that I depreciate style. In a Hawthorne I enjoy the grace and ductility of language, but then Hawthorne has a forceful thought here and there, by way of variety ; and it may be it is this concession to old-fashioned tastes that draws me along. The James school is too 'superior' to do anything of the sort. It will put the dictionary on the rack for you with pleasure ; if you want more, well, it will answer with many regrets that what you desire is not in its line. And it must be admitted that anything like force would indeed be an odd anomaly in its pages. As Mr. Buchanan recently reminded us, it is exceedingly ill-bred to think, feel, or act strongly, according to the James code of manners.

I am afraid you are ill-bred, for, while you are comparatively negligent of style, you think forcibly, and would seem to feel forcibly, for you make the reader feel forcibly ; and what say Horace and Mr. Walter Besant on that matter ? Mr. Howells, to be sure, laughs at the idea that an author is ever moved by his own work. But then it might be questioned whether Mr. Howells's laugh is conclusive on the point. There are scenes in *The Deemster* and *A Son of Hagar* that could hardly have been written in cold blood. At any rate, I think it would be hard to read some of them in cold blood—that one, for instance, in which the blind Mercy Fisher and her child appear for the last time, or that other on the Tynwald Hill, when a father strikes himself to the heart in sentencing the son he loves to perpetual banishment, or that further one on the top of Orris Head, where the cousins fight to the death. These are one or two scenes from among many that might be named which I think might move even Mr. Howells. The death of Mercy Fisher is as pathetic as that of her betrayer, Hugh Ritson, is tragic, while the scene on the Tynwald Hill is a thing which once read of can never be forgotten. The integrity, the stern justice of the judge, and the agony of the father in cutting off, as it were, his own right arm, are admirably described.   I seriously do not think that Walter Scott or Victor Hugo has anything better.   Certainly neither ever rises to a greater tragic height.

But your strength does not lie so much in detached scenes as in 'the entirety of expression and the cumulative effect of many particulars working toward a common end.'   Like a true artist your study is to evolve character, not to present it in brilliant patches.   And the manner in which the characters of Hugh Ritson and Daniel Mylrea are unfolded is, throughout, masterly, and shows true sense of proportion as well as the continuous working of the imagination.   Your men are better than your women, though Mercy Fisher and Mona are well and naturally drawn.   Perhaps as you proceed you will pay more attention to your female characters, and thus give more sweetness with your strength.

And as you are still young, your future will be watched with interest by all who have the welfare of our English literature at heart.   You have shown that you are capable of great things;

you have also shown, or at least hinted, that your aims are as high as your talents. In a recent magazine article you wrote that, ' Already the world seems to be growing weary of feeble copies of feeble men and feeble manners. It wants more grit, more aim, more thought, and more imagination. . . . Dugald Stewart said that human invention, like the barrel organ, was limited to a specific number of tunes. The present hurdy-gurdy business has been going on a longish time. We are threatened with the Minerva Press over again, and the class of readers who see no difference between Walter Scott and John Galt. But, free of the prudery of the tabernacle and the prurience of the boulevard, surely the novel has a great future before it. Its possibilities seem to be nearly illimitable. . . . To break down the superstitions that separate class from class ; to show that the rule of the world is right, and that, though evil chance plays a part in life, yet that life is worth living, these are among the functions of the novelist.'

In truth the time seems ripe for energetic and aggressive action in extending the scope of the

novel. It has long enough conformed to antiquated models, and been a slavish caterer to
illiberal—to use no harsher word—tastes. But
it has not altogether been the fault of the unlucky novelist that so much of our fiction has
been, and is, 'a tawdry and hollow article suited
for immediate use and immediate oblivion.'
The blame must be shared by the public, and
to some extent also by its tutors the critics.
While conditions of life were perpetually changing, while civilisation was giving her luminous
and benignant impress to whole new continents,
while science, to borrow an expressive phrase
from Mr. Gladstone, was progressing by leaps
and bounds, while the stream of general knowledge, swollen by new streams and unexpected
confluents, was overflowing all ancient boundaries, and deluging the country of thought far
and wide, the venerable standards of fiction,
surviving mutation and vicissitude, remained as
fixed and unalterable as the laws of the Medes
and Persians, and the unhappy novelist had the
choice of conforming or starving. Being human,
he preferred to have bread, and so art suffered.
But there are signs of a change; better things

seem to be in store for us, and the fact that *The Deemster* has enjoyed a fair measure of popularity shows a hopeful tendency in public taste.

A great deal has been and is being written about realism and romance, as if the two were divided by a fence, or as if great writers were not realistic and romantic by turns, and when it suited them. And it is certain that in giving the novel a wider scope, the novelist will press both realism and romance into his service, for in each lie essences of humanity which he cannot well neglect. But I fancy, though I express an opinion with all diffidence, that pure romance can scarcely ever regain the position it once occupied, and I should be inclined to regard the phenomenal success of certain recent exploits in the way of revival rather as confirming than contradicting this view. The diffusion of intelligence, the progress of science, the greater familiarity with, and better comprehension of, the phenomena of Nature, the keen, mechanical, materialistic bent of the age (I speak in no theological sense) seem to me fatal to the supremacy of pure romance. The most potent accessories to illusion are gone. Superstition no longer stalks at large to assist and stimulate the imagination. Faith is dying, and a spirit of haughty agnosticism is abroad. The same power which increases our material comforts diminishes our imaginative pleasures. Nature, in bestowing one talent, demands the surrender of another, and this exchange and barter, if beneficial on one side, is inimical on the other. We are not in all respects the same as our fathers have been. We are more cultured than they were, more sceptical, more cynical, and (in our own estimation at least) harder to impose on. It would be absurd to predict that we shall never have another great romance on the lines of *Ivanhoe* or *Don Quixote.* To genius all things are possible. Given a Titan and we shall have titanic achievements. But the fact that once upon a time Samson walked placidly off with the Gates of Gaza hardly warrants us in expecting to see the performance repeated. The feat of writing romance in the old sense is daily becoming more and more difficult, and not less from the change in the writer himself than from the altered attitude of the audience. The imagination of a cultured man is apt to cower before his intellect, ashamed of its airy nothings; and if in so recent a figure as Goethe we see the highest culture and the boldest imagination working in unison we but behold the exception that proves the rule.

The great novel of the future is likely to steer a middle course between Scylla and Charybdis. It will combine the best elements of realism and romance. The coming novelist will do away with all arbitrary limitations. Remembering that the primitive element in man is never wholly eradicated, he will not neglect the romantic, he will not disdain to minister to the emotions; and, always conscious of the forward march of the world, the passing away of so many old things, and the advent of so many new, he will strive to give æsthetic expression to the manners and forms of life about him. But he will copy nature as an artist, not as a photographer, and he will take of the temporary only what tends to illustrate the perennial. He has no right to be a bald historian or chronicler of small talk, or scientist, or political economist, **or even** a philanthropist **except in so far as** the best art is always phil-anthropic.   His mission will be to exhibit human motives and passions under **the** new lights of the new times.   **He will delight** in **novel** situations.   He will **not shrink from** showing human frailty; but he will not gloat **over it nor** divorce it from the virtues by which, save **in rare and** exceptional cases, it is **accompanied.**   And above all and beyond all, he will **not** forget that **it is of man's soul to** man's soul he is speaking.   **You, I believe, keep this in mind, and it is** mainly because **of this that** you have done **so** well in the past, and give **so rich a promise for the future.**

ROBERT LOUIS STEVENSON.

To Mr. ROBERT LOUIS STEVENSON.

Sir,—Your countryman, Carlyle, has said that 'could ambition always choose its own path, and were will in human undertakings synonymous with faculty, all truly ambitious men would be men of letters.' Not only have you chosen the envied path, but you are treading it with very eminent success. A very wide circle of readers is waiting impatiently to catch your every word, if not quite as if you were a Delphic oracle pouring out celestial wisdom, at least as if you were a wizard that could for a little charm them into forgetfulness of the fret and fume of this feverish life. Moreover, the critics are almost unanimously with you, more unanimously perhaps than with any other British author of the day, certainly far more unanimously than with any of our younger authors; so that it may be justly said you have conquered, and are fairly entitled to the honours and the spoils of the victor—to the laurel crown and the golden guineas, or, as vulgar people say, to the pudding and the praise.

It is no mean achievement to make a name in English letters even to-day; for despite the dolorous croaking of pessimists, and the sapient head-shaking of octogenarians, filled with fables of the past, there is really a good deal of literary talent in England at present. If she has fewer intellectual giants than in ages that are gone, the average stature is incomparably greater. If no Hamlets or Tom Joneses or Kenilworths are being produced, we turn out manufactures in every way superior to the Oliver Twists and the Pelhams of a preceding generation. So long as we have men like yourself labouring in the realm of fiction we may hold up our heads with self-respect, and feel that our appearance, if not very portly or imposing, is at least eminently respectable. We might be out of place in a chariot, but we are quite equal to the dignity of a gig.

Public men, it was long ago observed, are public property; this is peculiarly the case with authors. I do not exceed my proprietary rights, then, in glancing briefly at what you have accomplished, and examining the ground whereon your fame rests. You have been active in many departments. According to your own statement you have written innumerable dramas, which have never seen the light. Presumably they were not worth publishing ; for it is not your habit to withhold anything that could be of any possible interest to your literary admirers. So considerate are you in this respect, indeed, that at an early age you have given the world personal memoirs such as most authors reserve either for posthumous publication, or for publication at the very close of their careers. But there is no valid reason in the world why an author should not publish his memoirs when it suits him ; and the time is perhaps at hand when a writer will make his first appeal to the public with a volume of gossip about his baby playmates, and the troubles of teething - time. Your memoirs, though not without a touch of egotism, as some think, are so interesting that we shall be glad to have more when you have matter and leisure.

Your chief work, however, has been in the

realms of poetry, criticism, and romance. I dare say you would yourself be readiest to acknowledge that, if you had not been first favourably known as a prose writer, your poetry would hardly have gained you recognition. You have publicly attributed your success to your dire industry; and it is in reading your poetry rather than your prose that we see how just is your estimate of your own endowments. 'An infinite capacity for taking trouble' does not always fitly take the place of inspiration. In your *A Child's Garden of Verses* there are many neat, sweet, and happy little things suited to the tender age of childhood, but nothing, or very little, that would prove nutritious at a maturer period of life. I do not mean to imply that the book is aught but what it should be. It is excellent of its kind, only that kind is hardly high enough to justify one in giving you the title of poet. In *Underwoods* you take a more ambitious flight, and as ambition, while carrying a man triumphantly over many obstacles, exhibits his weakness no less than his strength, so in this book the limitations of your genius are sharply emphasised. Throughout the volume the mighty impress of Burns, to quote a phrase from Mr. Lowell, is distinctly visible. Like Shakespeare, Burns is so exceedingly natural that we are often betrayed into the self-delusion of imagining that what he has done with such apparent ease we also can do. The number of dramatists that the Stratford poacher has made is probably beyond computation, and Scotland is overrun with minor poets who would never have sung a note but for the Ayrshire ploughboy. You are, of course, a man of too wide a culture to limit yourself to a single model, nor would your sense of fitness ever permit you to go wholly on the lines of one who must ever remain, more or less, an alien to the great mass of the English people. Burns can never be thoroughly appreciated by Englishmen, and it is to Englishmen that you especially appeal. Still, in *Underwoods*, the influence of Burns is paramount, particularly in what I may call the personal section of the book. In short the work is imitative, and hardly takes high rank for originality. Perhaps it was merely a *tour de force*. If so, we may read it and enjoy it, and lay it aside, treating it in no more serious spirit than did the author.

In criticism you show to more advantage. To be sure, you are not absolutely without bias, and a biased critic is not to be implicitly trusted. You have called *Tom Jones* dull; and thereby drawn down on yourself the solemn admonitions of Mr. Augustine Birrell, and the sportful and partial anger of your friend, Mr. Andrew Lang. We cannot let you call the work of Henry Fielding dull and rank you as a great critic. But you have made amends for this little fantasy by being judicial in other directions.

Your judgments on Scott, and Dumas, and Victor Hugo, and Hawthorne, are, in the main, just; you have sufficient perspicacity to see, and sufficient candour to acknowledge, that Zola is not a blockhead; and you have courageously condemned the moral delinquencies of your poetic model, Burns. But while you have done something in verse, and given us one or two volumes of agreeable criticism, your true sphere is fiction. It is on your romances that you would yourself rest your claim to fame; and it is as a writer of romance that you are most widely known and most warmly admired.

When *Kidnapped*, which, I understand, you

consider your 'best, indeed your only good, story,' was published, one enthusiastic journal said it was as good as anything in Carlyle, and far truer. I confess the aptness of the remark did not strike me on perusing the book; but that is of little consequence. Another journal, equally generous, called it as good as *Rob Roy*. This last was very high praise indeed, and must have been peculiarly gratifying to you for three reasons—first, because the journal which gave the verdict was one of weight and influence; second, because you place Scott at the head of all writers of romance; and, third, because *Rob Roy* is, on your own confession, an especial favourite of yours. That you could wholly agree with the verdict, however, is more than I believe; for you can hardly imagine yourself just yet entitled to share Sir Walter's pedestal.

For myself, on reading *Kidnapped* I did not think it quite as good as *Rob Roy*. But I thought that for a boy's book, it was in many respects too good—that your fine gift of characterisation was virtually thrown away; for as you once observed yourself, boys do not care much for the study of character. If they did there would be but a poor chance for some books which are enjoying considerable popularity. It struck me, then, that your study of character was too fine, especially your study of the character of Alan Breck Stewart. But while thinking this, the manner in which that gentleman is drawn gave me the keenest delight. 'Here,' I said to myself, curiously enough, anticipating Mr. Augustine Birrell,—'here we have another splendid portrait added to the gallery of Scottish heroes of fiction.' That was my first impression. Further reflection, however, brought an ugly suspicion that the portrait was not entirely original after all; that, in fact, it had merely been taken down and touched up according to the latest canons in art. I felt as if I had met the redoubtable Alan Breck somewhere before; in other vestments, it is true, and engaged in other pursuits, but surely the same man. Where had I seen him? Was it in some previous state of existence, or only in a dream of the night? Sudden as a flash came the revelation. To be sure I had seen either him or his double before,—once when he was surreptitiously lifting his neighbour's cattle, and again

when he was holding complacent argument,—
like the daring rascal that he was—with a magi
strate in the Tolbooth of Glasgow. 'Ah, eh, oh!'
I exclaimed, falling, in my surprise, into the manner and dialect of the worthy Bailie Nicol Jar-
vie. 'My conscience, it's impossible—and yet
—no! conscience it canna be; and yet again—
Deil hae me! that I should say sae, ye robber,
ye cateran—ye born deevil that ye are to a' bad
ends and nae gude ane—can this be you?' and
calmly came the laconic rejoinder. 'E'en as
ye see.' I may be mistaken, but it certainly
seems to me that the lineaments of Mr. Stewart
too distinctly suggest those of Mr. Macgregor.
However, while saying this, let me hasten to
confess that I think *Kidnapped* the most delightfully written boy's book which has appeared
for at least a decade. It is the work of one
who is an artist, and not a mere sensation-
monger.

Of *Prince Otto* likewise one must speak with
qualification. It is full of charming writing,
but the characters are occasionally shadowy,
and no amount of literary decoration will
make a work of fiction tolerable in which the

characters are not under all circumstances and at all times thoroughly alive. The reader scarcely succeeds in getting into sympathy either with the fantastic prince or his scheming wife; and it is hard to believe that you ever were in thorough sympathy with them yourself. There is one part of the book, however, that could scarcely be improved, and that is the description of the flight of the Princess Seraphina when she finds the game up and the palace on fire. There is something like real inspiration in that passage. The picture of the conflagration, and the wretched flying woman remains with the reader long after he has forgotten all else.

Of *The Black Arrow* it is better I should not speak, for I hold that an author should be judged by his best performances, not by his worst.

Besides novels and tales you have written short stories, in which you have done yourself perfect justice. With the single exception of Mr. Thomas Hardy, no living British writer so well understands, or so well succeeds in, this extremely difficult branch of fiction as yourself. But here again we have to be on our guard against superlatives and false standards. The short story does not flourish in these Islands. They do these things better not only in France, but among our own kinsmen in America. Comparisons, as Dogberry sagely observed, are odorous, indeed they are malodorous, and I will not mention names; but I dare say you would be among the first to admit that so far as short stories are concerned British authors are not in the running with their Transatlantic brethren. Nevertheless your stories are distinctly good. *Thrawn Janet* is a first-class 'bogle' story of the kind one might hear any winter's evening by the ingle of a Scottish farmer or peasant, and *The Merrymen* never lacks interest if it sometimes lacks probability.

And now, just a word regarding your work in general. Mr. Andrew Lang has stated that, since Thackeray, no Englishman of letters has been gifted with, or has acquired, so charming or original a style as yours. That is substantially true. Your style is facile, quaint, and suggestive: often it is brilliant and always distinctive. Moreover, it has that subtle charm which lures one on one knows not how. In drilling yourself in the art of the novelist you have studied widely, and one sees in your work the influence of many masters. You have borrowed something from Hugo, from Dumas, from Scott, from Poe, from Hawthorne, and many others. But in the matter of style you are chiefly indebted to Hawthorne—the best stylist, to my mind, in the entire range of that huge mass of fiction which is widely styled English. To say that your style resembles his is no more than the truth. There are parts of *Prince Otto* which Nathaniel Hawthorne might have written; especially might he have written that part, already referred to, which describes the flight and the bitter feelings of the Princess Seraphina. That I think is your high watermark so far as style goes, and to say that it is worthy of the author of *The Scarlet Letter* is but to say that it would be hard to match it in contemporary literature.

Nor in the enumeration of your qualities should your humour be forgotten. Nothing is rarer in literature than true humour; and in these days of spasmodic and dreary jesting, when the Comic Muse so often presents the appearance of a draggled and broken-winded jade—when her skirts are so often foul with the mire of the slums, and her breath hot with the fumes of the pot-house, it is pleasant to meet her in her native state, — trim, light, graceful, and clean, — a shepherdess in her laughing robes. Your humour is genuine and spontaneous, and pervades all you write. It does not show itself in caricature, nor in horse-play, but rises naturally from the heart of the matter like a gushing spring from the hard rock to refresh the thirsty wayfarer. It is in your humour that you are most original, and perhaps most delicious.

To Mr. ANDREW LANG.

Sir,—If shades be capable of envy, and one sees no reason for doubting their capacity in that way, that of the late Mr. Crichton, sometime student at St. Andrews, must occasionally have a rather uncomfortable time of it. To be poet, critic, sportsman, wit, student, and professor of Folk Lore, confidant and biographer of fairies, novelist, parodist, anthropologist, magazinist, journalist, humorist, and many other -ists besides was not given to the most versatile of foregoing men. He has, indeed, a tolerable record in languages, if his history be not a fable, or a 'muckle white lee,' as his own and your countrymen would say; but in literature his performances were, after all, insignificant. Possibly the dolorous ghost might complain, if it condescended to discuss the point at all, that opportunities were scantier in the good old days than in these degenerate ones ; that disputations

ANDREW LANG.

in colleges were not so favourable for the display of mental power as the columns of the daily, weekly, and monthly press. And perhaps the ghost would be right. The world, on reliable authority, is moving forward; opportunities are on the increase. And there is of course a corresponding increase in the power and ingenuity of man. Every son of Adam progresses of sheer necessity. Darwinism has proved that he cannot stand still; nor can he go back to his roost and caudal appendage, which ought to be a consoling reflection. He is being constantly 'evolved,' much as the ingenious novelist evolves a character. Fresh faculties are, perhaps, added; at the very least old ones, which have lain dormant since the days of our arboreal ancestors, are developed and sharpened so as to perform functions that are essentially new. Hence it is that the pretensions of the Admirable Crichtons of the past can hardly be matter for serious consideration to-day. One would think that the estimable geniuses of other days must have something of the thankful feeling of Sir Walter about having lived in 'the early days of tradition,' when literary claims were not so narrowly scanned as they are to-day, and when versatility, not to speak of universality, was practically a thing unknown. At any rate it has been reserved for this wondrous century, which has witnessed so many striking phenomena, to mark with admiration the achievements of one whose only imperfections might seem to be that he is too sparing of sentiment, and somehow disinclined to do justice to 'M. de Howells' and his sturdy compatriots.

Philosophers are wont to observe that man is necessarily the creature of his age. None can escape the influence of his time. Shakespeare could not, nor Dante, nor Homer; and how should lesser men expect to succeed where the Titans failed? You are part of your age, yet not entirely of it. In some ways you are a more satisfactory representative of the latter half of the nineteenth century than the Rev. Robert Elsmere himself. He represents its narrowness; you represent its breadth, its many-sided culture, its neat and dainty universality. Our Time has as many arms as Briareus, and can use them all with equal ease and equal facility. You are 'grave and gay, lively and severe,' trifling and trenchant, as the need arises, and one never catches you in a *rôle* which you do not play to perfection. You not only do your 'level best' at all times and under all circumstances, but your level best is so good that one could hardly wish it better. In all this you represent your age; for despite a great deal of violent assertion to the contrary, thoroughness is not unknown. Where you do not represent your age is in its propensity to stoop. I am inclined to think that, notwithstanding your 'infinite capacity for taking trouble,' there is not much of the grubbing Teuton in you. You have more of the light and sportful spirit of Ariel, than the heavy, dull respectability and conscientiousness of purpose which we value so much in the adorable Dryasdust. The good creature is useful, he has a great talent for going to the bottom of things, but unhappily he often remains there; he is the dray-horse of literature, fit for drawing heavy loads over cobble-stones; your sphere is in the upper regions, where the movement is swift and graceful, and whence there is a comprehensive view without danger of contamination.

One sees in you the odd anomaly of a
romantic scientist, or a scientific romancist—
which you will, a polished scholar who loves and
clings to the barbarous element in humanity,
a shrewd man of the world who might be
more than half suspected of a lingering belief
in certain pleasant superstitions regarding the
supernatural and other kindred things, which
are usually objects of contempt to the enlightened man about town. On the critical side
none is keener, on the romantic or imaginative
few more credulous or blindly extravagant. On
occasion you can assume the callous, cold-
blooded manner of Matthew Arnold with an
appearance of perfect naturalness. You can
deal with the scientific novel in a scientific spirit,
and with the theological novel with a superficial look of delight, as if you really relished
rattling among the dry bones in the desolate
valley. But the enjoyment *is* superficial, for
the occupation, I take it, is not much to your
taste. You are fonder of following the vagaries
of Walter Scott than of working out the perplexing problems of the realist and the theologian.
One can imagine you throwing yourself on the

sofa, after the style of a certain idle reader, and exclaiming : 'Be mine to read eternal novels by Walter Scott.' You write of brownies, bogles, water-kelpies, border-feuds and forays with more fervour than of the spiritual struggles of Deacon Boozle, or the minute investigations of the heart troubles of Miss Jemima Mildjoy, of Boston, Mass. You have a keener relish of Homer and Haggard than of the school which describes life 'as it is.' Yet here again you are odd, for you have defended good Henry Fielding against the attacks of Mr. Stevenson, and admitted—perhaps reluctantly and regretfully, but still made the admission—that Mr. Henry James has accomplished the phenomenal feat of writing three or four really interesting novels about 'the young person' of the capital of New England. This shows that you can appreciate the beauty and utility of the microscope and the scalpel—with an effort. But admiration for the thew and sinew of manhood, the spear and battle-axe, would seem to be in the blood with you. Vigorous, buoyant, downright, above all successful, slaughter thrills you with a grateful sense of satisfaction, perhaps because in that particular you like thoroughness, while dissection or vivisection would seem to leave only an impression of petty sacrilege, or cruelty. And to be sure, Sir Henry Curtis hewing down rebellious Africans is a more imposing spectacle than Silas Lapham undergoing an examination of his emotional machinery. Every man to his taste. Some are born heroic, some realistic, and there really seems to be room enough in the world for both classes.

I have long thought that you are somewhat too severe on our Transatlantic friends. To the dead, indeed, you have done full justice. Hawthorne has had your discriminating praise, so has Poe, so has Longfellow. But the living cannot boast of it save in the minutest fragments. The robust young man from Topeka, Kansas, in top-boots, buckskin, and sombrero, has little but your sarcasm. He is an innovation in literature, and you do not seem to take to him kindly. I do not know whether you have studied Cousin Jonathan at home; I should fancy, from the vigour of your prejudices against him, you have not; but if you will take the word of one who has 'been there,' he is really a very fine fellow—in his own way. To be sure he has his imperfections—a good crop of them ; who has not ? He is brawny and uncouth, and his spirits are sometimes too boisterous for the sedate and the delicate. Besides, he is not without conceit. He makes himself out to be taller than he really is, and pretends a total indifference to British opinion. In reality, however, the dear fellow is very fond of England, likes to visit it, and is extremely sensitive to English criticism. It hurts him when you sit on him. And I do not know that it is good policy to laugh at him too much. Washington Irving—the most genial spirit in American literature—long ago pointed out the danger of treating America as if she were in every way—mental, moral, and social—an inferior ; and a living author, whose pride or patriotism is not greater than his general excellence as a writer, has complained that Americans are treated too much like children or clowns by John Bull.

Moreover, it seems to me that on purely intellectual grounds you scarcely mete out justice to the Americans. Every man has a weak point, most men have many such points, and to some it might appear that your weakness lies in what I may call your American side. There is much to be said against the Americans as a people, as there must be against any people so young, so strong, so prosperous, and with such an unexampled retrospect and prospect—much to be said if one cared, or it were profitable to say it. But if they have their deficiencies, they have likewise their merits, and all that they would ask for themselves is that those merits be impartially considered. 'We must submit ourselves to the European standard of weights and measures,' says Mr. Lowell. 'That we have made the hitherto biggest gun might excite apprehension (were there a dearth of iron), but can never exact respect. That our pianos and patent reapers have won medals does but confirm us in our mechanical and material measure of merit. We must contribute something more than mere contrivances for saving of labour, which we have been only too ready to misapply in the domain of thought and the higher kinds of invention. In those Olympic games, where nations contend for truly immortal wreaths, it may well be questioned whether a mowing-machine would stand much chance in the chariot races ; whether a piano, though made by a chevalier, could compete successfully for the prize of music.' They demand only simple justice, and, to my mind, it is only simple justice to let them have it. It is curious that you, who have generally such an open eye for all kinds of excellence, whether it be of the grave or gay sort, should be so persistently 'down' on the Americans, who, I think, have at present amongst them some first-rate artists. I do not think that it requires any effort—at least I have never found it anything else than a great pleasure—to read the novels of, let us say, Mr. Cable or Miss Murfree. And in regard to criticism, I read the 'Editor's Study' in *Harper's,* and 'At the Sign of the Ship' in *Longman's,* with the same profit and delight. As a certain poet says, 'Oh wad ye tak' a thocht an' men'' in that American business. The sarcasm which is so keen, so cutting, so destructive, so entertaining, would not then be under the suspicion of occasional unfairness.

For the rest, what is one to say? That if you are not precisely the first of existing English writers, you are by far the most versatile. I think the statement might be seriously made, and still keep on good terms with truth and conscience. There may be writers who are more trenchant—force is not, perhaps, your forte; there may be those who tear the heart out of a subject more pitilessly; there may even be a few who are more diverting; but I cannot at present recall the name of one who goes round the entire circle of intellectual activity with greater apparent ease, or more consummate grace. From Herodotus to Hawthorne, from Theocritus to Thackeray, from Homer to Mr. Rider Haggard, from Lucretius to Longfellow, from the Customs of Primitive Man to the Curiosities of Parish Registers, you glide with easy and fascinating mastery. In most men this versatility would be fatal. The productions of ' the mob of gentlemen who write with ease' are not always, as Sheridan pointed out, the easiest reading in the world. Not infrequently they are a sore tax on patience. But you have yet to learn the art of disappointing us. It is an art which, unfortunately, most writers master comparatively early in life, and go on practising with an assiduity and success that are occasionally too much for the most friendly of readers. But you, whether we agree with you or not (and I may say that, on many things, your views are not mine), are always interesting in the sense in which Mr. Haggard's young lady would use that word. Wherein lies the magic? In the subjects you choose? As often as otherwise they are perfectly commonplace in themselves. 'I heard the Rev. Henry Ward Beecher the other night,' said Mr. Sala once. 'I was delighted with him, and didn't agree with a word he said.' What is this magic that charms without convincing? It clearly lies in the man, and not in the matter.

One cause of your success with cultivated readers is, undoubtedly, that you are primarily a poet. There is something of the sunshine of the fancy in all you write, even your most hurried notes. The harp is struck carelessly— no, not carelessly, but lightly, and often there is only a passing note of music, but, like the 'Mesopotamia' of Whitfield, it never fails to fetch the reader. Another reason for your success is that you are a humorist; and still another, that you are never too much in earnest. Earnest people are often rude, often tread, and not always by accident, on the toes of their best friends. We should as soon expect clumsiness from M. Daudet, or cleanliness from M. Zola, as rudeness from you. You can be stern, you can be keen, you can hit mercilessly in the joints of the harness, but your manner will always be unimpeachable. You have called Mr. Norris the successor of Thackeray. Will you allow me to say that, of all living writers, you seem to me to come nearest the great master's manner. That rare penetration, that perfect lucidity of thought, that light, yet effective style, which seems merely sportive at the first glance, yet cuts like a Damascus blade, which belonged to Thackeray, belong also to you. But I confess there are times when it seems to me Thackeray might have hit straighter from the shoulder with advantage. An honest knock-down blow is a thing to admire, and be grateful for on occasion. You are not, any more than was the author of the *Roundabout*

Papers, a Hercules—that is, you are averse to the use of the club, when the club might be more serviceable than the lighter weapons of offence. One would like to see you 'tremendously in earnest' a little oftener. One would like to see you take hold of the more serious problems of life in a more serious spirit at times. We may live in Mayfair now, but it will not always be so. Life may have much comedy in it, but it has more of tragedy, and there are times when persiflage is barely tolerable. Sentiment is a bad thing to parade, but we like a writer at times to make us feel that he has got a little of it in the closet. You have just a trifle too much of the gift of self-repression, which is so needful to an artist, and yet so fatal when exercised to excess. One often thinks that if you had a touch of sentiment to make your brilliancy mellow, you would be the most charming of modern writers.

That you are capable of seriousness no one who has read you will for a moment doubt. Perhaps no more convincing instance could be given of this little-known characteristic of your literary genius than the sonnet with which you preface your translation of the *Odyssey*. I consider it one of the most beautiful things in recent literature :—

' As one that for a weary space has lain,
      Lulled by the song of Circe and her wine,
      In gardens near the pale of Proserpine,
  Where that Ææan isle forgets the main,
  And only the low lutes of love complain,
      And only the shadows of wan lovers pine,
      As such an one were glad to know the brine
  Salt on his lips, and the large air again,—
  So gladly, from the songs of modern speech
      Men turn, and see the stars, and feel the free
  Shrill winds beyond the close of heavy flowers,
  And through the music of the languid hours
  They hear, like ocean on a western beach,
      The surge and thunder of the Odyssey.'

A little more in that high, free spirit would be very grateful.

WILLIAM DEAN HOWELLS.

To Mr. WILLIAM DEAN HOWELLS.

Sir,—Up to the date of the latest literary intelligence from the West the Great American Novel, so often announced with a triumphant blare of trumpets from various centres of enlightenment throughout the Republic, and ever postponed for certain mysterious, but, doubtless, satisfactory reasons—this promising and much desiderated work, in which we are to have a full and faithful presentation of the heterogeneous elements of American life, from Alaska to New Orleans, from Maine to California, has not yet made its appearance. Until it shall have been written, or, at any rate, until it shall have been published, it would be something of an exaggeration to style any American writer truly national. In a literary congress of the world America could accredit no single individual to represent her. The representation would have to be by districts, as if Transatlantic authors could attain only to the dignity of being parochial representatives, and all owing to the delay in publishing that book. Why is its publication so long deferred? What is wanting for a consummation so devoutly to be wished as a full-length portrait of the fair and spacious giantess, who on one side cools herself in the surf of the Atlantic, and on the other suns herself along the golden Pacific? To outsiders, like myself, not acquainted with matters of internal policy, the question is pertinent and interesting, and the failure of the authorities to answer it might beget doubt of the ability of Transatlantic writers to cope with the subject. We frequently hear of the splendid opportunities of the American novelist. The freshness of his materials, we are told, the fluidity of the social state, the sharp contrasts of manners and complexions afford an artist a chance of making a picture of unmatchable magnificence and impressiveness; but the picture itself has not, so far as I am aware, yet reached these shores. It would be idle to say that we have any satisfactory likeness of the giant nation lying within the boundaries of the United States. Delightful Vignettes, indeed, we have in plenty; for the American artist, if not always, so virile or robust as one could wish, is rarely lacking in deftness. We have glimpses of the Republic and her people, which are often beautiful, and not infrequently suggestive and stimulating. Mr. Lowell, with rare and consummate art, gives us that singular combination of worldly shrewdness and moral fervour—rural New England; Mr. Bret Harte, with almost unmatched dramatic power, draws California in her shirt sleeves, if I may be permitted to use the expression—a pick in one hand and a pack of cards in the other; Louisiana has her laureate in Mr. Cable, and Tennessee in Miss Murfree; Ole Virginia and Georgia have skilful and sympathetic delineators in Mr. Stockton and Mr. Joel Chandler Harris; while Boston, the Hub of the Universe, as Dr. Holmes facetiously called it, has had ample attention at the hands of Mr. Henry James and yourself. Thus we have sketches in abundance; but the finished and organic picture, which should fitly present the multitudinous and diverse elements which constitute the national life we have not.   And why? one is again tempted to ask.   Is it that the American novelist is abashed by the dimensions of the subject?   Beyond question it is a large one, and one, moreover, requiring no ordinary mental power, if it were to be treated as it ought.   Perhaps, indeed, only a Shakespearian amplitude of intellect were equal to its demands, for it embraces not only America proper, but Europe, Asia, and Africa as well.   The great American Novel when it does, in the course of the centuries, arrive will be a phenomenal, an un-paralleled book.   I do not expect to have the pleasure of perusing it.   Nor, considering its universal scope, am **I** altogether sorry; for if writers have their limitations, so, also, have readers; and too vast a book cannot but prove a great weariness of both flesh and spirit.

· America, then, has hitherto produced no writer who, in any strict sense, could be called truly representative; but this much, I think, might truthfully be said, that, of all her writers, none is more truly representative than yourself.

Not only have you depicted, with inimitable grace and unmatched fulness, certain characteristic features of American life, but you show fewer traces of foreign influence—at least of British influence—than any other American writer I could at present name. While most of your writing compatriots have been eager to display their tincture of European culture (and European culture in America generally means English culture), you have stood manfully on your instincts, and stuck to your plain Republic. In this, as I have said, you are almost alone ; for a thin cosmopolitanism is at once the ambition and the vice of American men of letters. Even so sturdy a patriot as Mr. Lowell, whose pen has so often and so eloquently defended his country and poured a withering sarcasm on her enemies and detractors, has expressly stated that in literature, at least, America must take example by England. You assert the contrary, and not only assert it, but practise it. Things of indigenous growth are good enough for you. Boston, in your estimation, may vie with Athens, and New York would seem to have tastes infinitely superior to those of London. Perhaps, æsthetically, Chicago is above Edinburgh.

The English people are obviously little to your mind. If we are to judge from your books, you consider them always arrogant, and often not a little insolent. Their conceit would seem to be quite unmatchable, their modes of thought to be antiquated, their views insular and narrow, their novels mostly absurd, their criticism entirely contemptible. When you notice them, it is chiefly to contradict and deride. When you want the weight of an authoritative name, you do not choose from their considerable list ; you pass them by contemptuously, and give your patronage to France, or Italy, or Russia. You so far bow to tradition, indeed, as to speak with approval of Shakespeare ; you even borrow from him on occasion, as witness some of your titles ; but as a rule, when you are in the mood to admire, you give British authors a wide berth, and British critics a still wider one.

It were of course vain to quarrel with you for all this. I trust I am as good a patriot as my neighbours, and should as little like to see my country menaced or my countrymen maligned, but candour must admit that there is a measure, a considerable measure, of truth in many of your strictures on questions affecting English literature and English taste. I think it was Emerson who said that a man of character likes to be told of his faults; and I am sure that the English nation, as a whole, has character enough to receive your reproofs in a spirit profitable for edification, and not only that, but to admire your unswerving pertinacity and your sturdy independence. On matters of taste, it is perfectly clear that no oracle can be final and conclusive; and it is not to be expected that the British people will cast aside the convictions which come of the accumulated experience of centuries of high and earnest endeavour to embrace doctrines which, however admirable in their way, and however potent for good in some communities, would often have little to recommend them here, except their novelty. The people of these Islands are, by temperament and tradition, conservative. They have a dread of what they style new-fangled notions, a dread so keen that they often reject valuable counsel, for no more logical reason than because it recommends innovations. This **is a failing which** really arises from a virtue. Conscious of a past which, in many respects, transcends in glory all that is recorded **of the** nations of antiquity, they feel with uncommon **acuteness** the weight of responsibility resting **upon them.** Their temper is to conserve at any **cost of sacrifice what has been** gathered and **built up by a brave and noble** ancestry ; hence **they are** too often blind to the opportunities and possibilities of the present. Like house-**holders** who have amassed a competency, they **are timid** in experimenting, lest experiment should endanger their possessions.

There can **be** no doubt whatever that **Eng-land has much to learn from America, not only in those manual and mechanical arts in** which **we are usually willing to** acknowledge our own inferiority, **but** in the higher spheres of intel-lectual **activity,** in which we are not so ready to **own** any real rivalry. And in this respect the **strictures** of a perspicacious critic like yourself **are invaluable. Let it be frankly admitted that** we are children of Adam, and have our shortcomings ; that England is not the world, far less the universe ; that our tastes are occasionally peculiar, and not always pre-eminently intelligent ; that our books are not immeasurably superior to the books of all other nations ; that our criticism would be none the worse of a trifle more breadth at times ; in a word, that we English are a fallible race, with serious limitations, and not a few robust prejudices ; and that we have not always shown that openness and generosity of mind in respect of the efforts and admonitions of Cousin Jonathan that would perhaps be becoming ; let all this be owned, and promises of amendment made.

On the other hand, it is possible that America, if she were inclined that way, might learn something from England. The mother-country is the older, and has the greater capital of experience ; moreover, her intellectual achievements are in reality more considerable than those of even her most stalwart daughter. Might it not be well to bear this in mind while animadverting on her performances ? To the general reader it is very entertaining to find critics, on either side of the Atlantic, indulging in caustic recriminations; but the judicious cannot but regret the presence of so acrimonious a spirit in international compliments. The Anglo-Saxon race should have other aims than to show its ingenuity in the elaboration of petty differences. Both England and America have so many good points, so many points in common, and they are both so strong, that they ought not to indulge in small squabbles. A spirit of chivalry is becoming in the high and powerful.

I have dwelt on this point at some length, because I think it of more importance than is generally conceived. Literature is so subtle, it is necessarily so pervasive of all our best thinking in every direction, that any infection, which is likely to prove generally injurious, should be especially guarded against. Besides, if you will pardon me for saying so, it is not for artists of your standing and talent to descend to the demeaning trade of the John Dennises. Healthy, hearty indignation is a thing to be admired, but the spirit of carping is an evil spirit, and to be avoided. Your skill is best exhibited in giving us such delicately-drawn characters as Lydia Blood and Egeria Boynton,

Constance Wyatt and Isabel March. Give us a little more of that feminine world, in delineating which you have hardly a living rival, and leave fault-finding to those whom Nature intended for the business.

Mr. Henry James has said somewhere that it is something for a novelist to have a plan, a theory. Assuredly it is, but it is a great deal more to give it artistic embodiment. It is not every writer who makes precept and practice agree. Now whatever adverse critics might say of you, and they have said a good many things, they could hardly call you inconsistent. Your theories of life and art may be open to objection ; it might be said they lack breadth, but no one could say that you preach one thing and practise another. You have very distinct ideas of what you wish to do, and you have the power, the rare and enviable power, of carrying out your conceptions. You have your limitations, perhaps they could easily be shown ; but as far as you go, you seem to me to have as easy a mastery over your materials as any of your contemporary novelists. Your ideals may not, in the eyes of some, be particularly lofty ;

but, so far as a reader can judge, you carry them out to the utmost. This gift of perfect expression is rare,—in reality, perhaps, the rarest in literature. Only a very few writers of all the ages give one the impression of being able, through literary mediums, to express precisely what they wish. Shakespeare has this power— as he has most powers of which man has any cognisance—so has John Bunyan, so has Defoe; and so, in our own time, have two very different men, Cardinal Newman and Mr. Lowell. The power, as I have said, is yours also. I do not know, I cannot imagine, how you would deal with the heroic. It is probable your keen critical sense and your intimate self-knowledge would keep you from attempting what Nature had not fitted you for. At any rate you have essayed nothing hitherto which you have not accomplished easily and well; so that if we might occasionally quarrel with your ambition, it would be unjust to impugn your power.

Your first characteristic, then, is clear-sightedness (the root, one would say, of most excellences which a writer can possess), and this is shown equally in your criticisms and your creations. It emphasises your merits and marks your limitations. Your comments on the Italian poets, for example, are as shrewd and keen as your analysis of the character of Professor Owen, or Silas Lapham; of Grace Breen, or Kitty Ellison. And in your criticism and your analysis alike, your compass is limited. In many ways you are a most peculiar writer. You see into your subject with uncommon clearness for a certain distance, but you come, all at once, as it were, to a blank wall, which completely shuts off the view, and cannot be scaled. I do not think your work gives much evidence of intuition. You yourself would deny that it gives any. And, certainly, what you do not actually see you seem unable to divine. And this, as I have said, is at once your excellence and your defect. As there is nothing vague in your writings, so there is not much that is majestic. Grandeur is not in your line. Your novels have been called the incarnation of the commonplace. In another sense than the critic intended, their highest merit is that they are truly and truthfully commonplace, that they depict the world as we see it about us, and depict it with exact and courageous fidelity. What we call impressiveness is, in most authors, oftener owing to defect than to perfection of vision. Dante, to be sure, can be impressive and minute—he is the greatest of all realists, but Milton to be impressive must be vague; and it is with the majority of writers as with Milton. We are impressed by Coleridge, by Richter, and sometimes by Hawthorne, without knowing precisely how or why; and we are convinced they could not themselves reveal the secret of their impressiveness. Thus much is imposing, simply because it is vague. Now you never have the advantage of dimness or gloom. Your characters are always in the full glare of the light. So soon as they pass out of the sunlight, they pass out of the reader's ken. They do not hover for an indefinite period in the twilight, duskily seen in the falling darkness, increasing in dimension in proportion as they diminish in distinctness. With you there is no duskiness, no debatable land. It is either white light or complete darkness. Hence, so far as it goes, everything is definite and unmistakable.

But, oddly enough, this very definiteness has given the impression that you are a superficial observer of your fellow-men, whereas the fact is there are few keener, few who see or feel with so much certainty within certain limits. Your creations, if they are seldom romantic and never heroic, are always intensely human. They may be commonplace characters (by commonplace, I presume, is meant people, such as we ordinarily meet in real life), but they are beyond all cavil creatures of flesh and blood, with the same ambitions, the same impulses, and pretty much the same foibles as ourselves. There is hardly one of them whom we do not come to know as thoroughly as we usually know our acquaintances in the world. Your women are especially admirable. I do not remember a single dim or ineffectual portrait in all your female gallery. Isabel March, Florida Vervain, Lydia Blood, and the rest of them are capitally drawn. All your grace, subtlety, and delicacy come out in your women, for you seem to be complete master of the variable feminine nature. I do not know that ladies have always cause to be grateful to you. You do not flatter them any more than does Mr. Hardy, but surely you do not libel them. At all events your portraits marvellously resemble many originals to be met daily in the world about us.

The delicacy which finds its fittest expression in the delineation of feminine character is also seen in your style. I have seen you censured for being fastidious and far-fetched in your literary expression. Even if the charge were just, it is surely better to be elegant and clean than slovenly and coarse as so many of our novelists are. But I do not think the indictment will hold. In speaking of your style, I think original would be a much more appropriate epithet than far-fetched; and no one with an eye or an ear for such things can deny that your writing is graceful and musical almost beyond example in the present day.

WILLIAM BLACK.

To Mr. WILLIAM BLACK.

Sir,—I sometimes try to imagine what the aspect of our English literature of the nineteenth century would be with the works of Scottish authors left out. I fancy the extent of the breach would astonish most people, assuredly it would astonish such as are in the habit of vaguely relegating intellect to the southern half of the kingdom. In poetry, indeed, the loss would be trivial if every line written by Scotsmen during the past ninety years were expunged ; for even Campbell and Scott do not stand in the first rank of poets, nor very high in the second, while the hordes of Wilsons and Aytouns and Tennants are scarcely to be reckoned as making any sensible contribution to the array of thought which constitutes our national British literature.

In criticism, history, and biography Auld Scotia does better ; for in these departments will be found the mighty names of Carlyle, Jeffrey, and Macaulay; but it is in fiction she does best, since in it she leads the nations.

One often wonders how the world could ever get along without the novels of Scott. How did the readers of the ages preceding his birth do without them?—without *The Bride of Lammermoor*, *Old Mortality*, *The Antiquary*—which so good a judge as Mr. Wilkie Collins considers the best novel ever written—and all the others left us by the same creative hand? To be sure, there were novelists before Scott. There was Fielding, brilliant, penetrative, humorous, virile, original, daring, often coarse, and sometimes positively indecent, it is true; yet, with all his faults, a writer to be proud of in even an Augustan age, and who has his admirers after the Wizard of the North has performed his wonders, and the author of *Kidnapped* pronounced *Tom Jones* dull. And there was Smollet, just a little less in stature than Fielding, stained too, but vigorous and entertaining; and Defoe, with his immortal *Crusoe*; and the solemn and sentimental Mr. Samuel Richardson; and Sterne, the finest humorist in all our literature, except Burns ; and Goldsmith, leading his gentle *Vicar,* whose passage from the blue room to the green is as interesting as most people's voyage round the globe ; and the sublime Mrs. Radcliffe with her *Mysteries of Udolpho*; and the great and gloomy Swift with his *Gulliver,* which still, perhaps, stands unrivalled for directness and force. But with all these one is again constrained to ask how our great-great-grandfathers and their elegant spouses got along without the novels of Scott, and how we should get along without them ? Carlyle asked quite seriously whether we would not rather part with our Indian Empire than with our Shakespeare ; and, if the choice had to be made, I dare say we should rather give up any considerable piece of territory than our Walter Scott.

That the greatest of all novelists should have been a Scotsman, and that Scotsmen still take the lead in fiction, is a matter of no little pride to the people of Scotland, and of no little interest to folks at large. The national character of the Scottish people is not popularly thought to be such as would tend to give them preeminence in that engaging art of lying, the decadence of which Mr. Oscar Wilde recently lamented. No doubt there are 'grand leears' among the Scotch as among other enlightened peoples ; but, as a whole, they are thought to be rather sternly and solemnly veracious, paying far more heed to hard fact, particularly when it takes the form of hard cash, than to flowers of fancy, however beautiful, or to creations of the imagination, however sublime. They are not romantic, but oppressively matter-of-fact ; in fact, they are the last people in the world whom we should suspect of sitting down to write 'idle and profane stories.' Yet, prosaic as they are, they are giving us the bulk of our best imaginative prose.

As you are one of the most popular of novelists now living, so, also, you are one of the best. You have, in my opinion, given us more interesting stories and finer studies of Scottish character than any other writer since the days of Scott, though Mrs. Oliphant's pictures of Scottish life are invariably excellent. But I think Mrs. Oliphant scarcely does herself justice. I fear she writes too much. The mass of literature she has produced is so stupendous that one is forced to sum up its merits as Macaulay did the work of Dr. Nares on *Burleigh and his Times*, by saying that it consists of so many thousand printed pages, that it occupies so many hundred inches, cubic measure, and that it weighs so many pounds avoirdupois. To be sure, Mrs. Oliphant invariably turns out good work. She does not scamp; but then she rarely concentrates herself upon any supreme effort. She is in such a hurry that she hardly takes time to fuse her characters in her mind, so that, while one would not hesitate to pronounce them well-drawn, there is still something hard and undeveloped about them ; and it is only by flashes and hints that we discern the real power of the writer, or what she might accomplish if she were less determinedly energetic. You have been truer to yourself. It would perhaps be impossible for a popular author to practise the reticence which alone ensures continuous artistic excellence, and I will not say you have not been guilty of over-production ; but, on the other hand, you have more than once bent all your faculties on a single book, and so done yourself and your readers justice. *A Daughter of Heth*, for instance, shows the artist master of his art. Mr. Shorthouse, indeed, places it in the very first rank of works of fiction, and says, ' It not only fulfils the requirements of the human spirit, but stands the more difficult test of being perfect as a whole.'

That is high praise, but it is not undeserved. The book grows naturally and organically, the characters are consistent and clearly drawn, there are both humour and pathos, and the descriptions are compact and graphic. *A Princess of Thule*, too, is a work of real art ; so, likewise, is *Macleod of Dare*, notwithstanding its unhappy ending. By the way, does it mar the artistic merits of a book to end unhappily, supposing such ending is logical and consistent ? I have heard readers express themselves as being delighted with all but the end of *Macleod of Dare*. What would they have ? Did they expect you to trample on logic, and thwart destiny by bringing your hero out pink and smiling ? Truly, there are some most un-reasonable people in this world. The end of

Macleod of Dare is the best piece of work you have ever done—nay, more, it is one of the best pieces of work done by any novelist, living or dead. There is inspiration in it, and I dare say you could not have averted the terrible fate of the hero if you would. And why should you if you could? Does life always, or even invariably, end in blissful sunshine? If not, then why should novels, which are supposed to be transcripts of life?

'Ah, but it is so very distressing to witness those catastrophes of unhappy endings,' says the languid creature, who wishes to be amused. Doubtless, but since Adam sinned, if we want to look on truth we must look on suffering. Had Eve not partaken of that unlucky apple, then all might have been different. In an ideal state, all novels should have happy endings, if, indeed, in the ideal state, people would care for anything so trivial as fiction. Other states— other tastes and amusements. Perhaps reality would have a greater attraction then.

But, indeed, this outcry against unhappy endings is inexpressibly silly; and it is well that a writer should occasionally please himself by taking his own way. **If it be** the right thing to **do, let him hang,** drown, **or** shoot his hero, regardless of censure. **A man** who is born for misery and a violent death has clearly no right to happiness and a peaceful exit. Nor should a heroine, born under an **adverse star, be** allowed to hug a husband or **fondle a baby.** These things **are for the fortunate only. At** the same time, **when** Fate is propitious, it were **folly to thwart her.** Weddings, after all, are, as **the young lady** observed, 'very nice things **indeed, and there can** hardly be too many of **them.'**

Your forte is the delineation of Highland character, which you understand well. Your Highlanders always **bear** the stamp of reality. One may meet them in the North any **day. It has been my lot to** mingle with Highlanders **pretty frequently, and I** must, in justice, say **that you draw the** Scottish Celt as he has not been drawn by any other living writer whatso-**ever.** Nor do you depend for your interest on the exceptional **and abnormal.** Your High-landers **are not Rob Roys and Alan Breck Stewarts. That** breed, thank heaven, is extinct, and in its place has grown up a class infinitely more heroic if less spectacular, though Southern critics do not always seem to be aware of the fact. It would be amusing, were it not so painful, to note the opinions which are still prevalent south of the Tweed regarding the people of the far North. Notwithstanding the facilities of travel, and the revolution which those facilities have worked in almost every department of knowledge, there is still a deplorable ignorance of the Highland character in enlightened England. This is not because Englishmen do not visit the northern half of Scotland, but because they are too lofty and precipitate in their methods of judging. The Highlanders are not to be understood in a day, nor in a week, nor even in a year. They are proud, shy, and sensitive, and do not readily reveal themselves to strangers, particularly to strangers who affect airs of superiority. A haughtier people than the Highlanders does not exist, and never did exist. Hospitable as are the Scottish Celts, a word or look is often enough to make them coil up within themselves like hedgehogs, and show only bristles that will prick if touched.

Above all, they cannot endure to be patronised ; so that, when glib literary tourists of the Joseph and Elizabeth Pennell species go north to air their conceit, their prepossessions, and their immeasurable ignorance, the poor Highlander, having some self-respect, keeps to himself, preferring even misrepresentation to the dire calamity of familiarity with such a set. The rubbish that has been printed about the Highlands and the Highlanders passes the bounds of imagination. There is something sublime in the easy audacity with which peripatetic critics, from the days of Samuel Johnson and Jamie Boswell down, pronounce judgment on the unfortunate inhabitants of the Highlands.

Had you done nothing else than write *A Princess of Thule* and *Macleod of Dare* you would have deserved well of your generation for courageously using your eyes and speaking the truth respecting a people that has been most cruelly misunderstood and misrepresented. The name of William Black rouses enthusiasm in the north and west of Scotland. The people there think that he at least understands and loves them ; and they are right, for

he does both.   Have you flattered them?
Surely not.   You have simply painted them as
they are, thereby once more proving that 'there
is nothing good or beautiful outside of what is
true, nothing noble or sacred outside of what is
natural.'

Into the question whether your work is in-
trinsically great, it were perhaps idle to enter,
seeing the world is so very uncertain in its own
mind respecting what constitutes real greatness.
You have truth and naturalness, and no incon-
siderable poetic power, and many would say
that these are in themselves the essence of greatness.   But you remember what Carlyle says of
the first of all novelists.   'Friends to precision
of epithet,' says the Sage of Chelsea, ' will probably deny his title to the name "great."   It
seems to us there goes other stuff to the making
of great men than can be detected here.   One
knows not what idea worthy of the name of great,
what purpose, instinct, or tendency, that could
be called great Scott ever was inspired with.
. . . There is nothing spiritual in him. . . .
Winged words were not his vocation; nothing
urged him that way; the great Mystery of

Existence was not great to him, did not drive him into rocky solitudes to wrestle with it for an answer to be answered or to perish. He had nothing of the martyr; into no dark region to slay monsters for us did he, either led or driven, venture down; his conquests were for his own behoof mainly, conquests over common market labour, and reckonable in good metallic coin of the realm. . . . Shall we call this great ? It seems to us there dwells and struggles another sort of spirit in the inward parts of great men.'

This is not the standard by which we judge our authors nowadays. Shall we apply it to you ? Shall we inquire what dark regions you have wrestled in, and what spiritual victories you have gained? Shall we inquire whether you have grown lean like Dante or Mahomet in your spiritual fights? or cast your inkstand at the devil like Martin Luther? Shall we throw your characters on the dissecting-table, and see whether there be any Othellos, or Hamlets, or Mignons among them? In a word, shall we, in strictest scientific method, proceed to probe and weigh you to ascertain whether in the old high sense you are a great man? The practice is really out of date. Time was when the transcendental philosopher Fichte might truthfully describe the man of letters as a priest interpreting, or endeavouring to interpret, Heaven's message to man. But that day has gone by. The world has changed, marched forward, as some think, and the man of letters has now other aims. Literature has become a profession, and is followed like any other, not for the purpose of 'revealing the God-like to man,' but for most part as the readiest means of securing a share of that good metallic coin of the realm of which Mr. Carlyle speaks so contemptuously. You do not concern yourself with the slaying of monsters. Readers will find few spiritual wrestlings in your novels, a fact for which on the whole they ought humbly to thank Heaven. Our spiritual and religious needs are being so well looked after by novelists, from Count Tolstoi to Mrs. Ward, that it is really something of a relief—a wicked pleasure some might call it—to read a novel in which the hero does not go through the agonies of religious doubt and despair, and in which the heroine is not made miserable by doctrines she does not understand. After all, foolish, erring, warm-blooded, passionate human nature is better than the dolorous things that issue, from time 'to time, from the shadows of our theological seminaries to wring the hands, to wail and tear the hair in public, as if their chiefest function were to exhibit their skill and ingenuity in making themselves wretched. The novelist's first concern, one would say, should be with humanity pure and simple. When human nature has been exhausted he might have a turn at theology, but in the meantime the majority of readers would be better pleased by his sticking to that desperately wicked and deceitful thing the heart. That you have generally been content with it is at once the ground of your excellence and the cause of your popularity.

ROBERT BUCHANAN.

To Mr. ROBERT BUCHANAN.

Sir,—You are perhaps the best existing type of the militant man of letters. Certainly none is readier to fight, none less awed by the quality of an opponent. You are not daunted by great names, nor restrained by considerations of policy. You donned your armour and furbished your blade as readily and joyously to meet the late Mr. Matthew Arnold as you now assume the fighting gear to meet Mr. Andrew Lang, or Mr. George Moore, or Mr. Edmund Yates, or Mr. Labouchere. The challenge never comes to you in vain ; nor are you to be disturbed with impunity. The thistle might well be engraven on your shield, and ‘ Ready, aye ready ’ would not be an inappropriate motto. Like the bold Macpherson, your literary life has been one of ‘ sturt and strife.’ From that early assault on ‘ The Fleshly School of Poetry ’ to the recent bombardment of ‘ Imperial Cockneydom,’ you have encountered many a doughty warrior, and dealt many a weighty and valorous blow. And the spirit of the fray is still strong upon you. To-day, as in times past, you present yourself with girded loins and an undiminished ardour for battle. I suppose there are times when you would really prefer not to fight, but the public knows nothing of you in such moments of weakness. So far as you are known to your readers, the arms are always in order, and the spirit ever eager.

I am disposed to think that it is not love of fighting for its own sake that leads you to unsheathe your sword so frequently, but a love of truth, a love of fair-play, a love of purity and goodness, a love of high principles and your fellow-men. You are not simply a polemic; though, once you are in the arena, you are as hot and stubborn a controversialist as the late Charles Reade himself. You do not seem, to me, to take up arms for the pleasure of destroying, or the glory of jumping on weak opponents. And certainly you do not take them up with an eye to your own profit. It is not by 'telling the truth and shaming the deil,' as the Scottish proverb has it, that

men gather in the shekels. Though it is painful to be compelled to make the admission,
rather the contrary is the case. 'If a man
would fill his granaries and attain to the sublime heights of worldly prosperity,' says a quaint
old moralist, 'three things he must earnestly
pray to be delivered from. He must petition,
first, that he be not stirred up to a vehement
insistence on disagreeable truths ; what men
profess to be deaf to let him be silent on :
second, that he be not tempted to cross the
vanity or self-love of his fellows ; for thereby
ensueth bitterness and strife which do mightily
hinder a man : third, that he be endowed with
the supple properties of the willow, which
bendeth gracefully before the blast ; for assuredly it cometh to pass that the man like the
tree that bendeth not shall be levelled by the
hurricane. The Gallic proverb, that there is
nothing beautiful but truth, containeth a griev-
ous heresy. Verily it is my opinion that this
same wench who is called truth hath been the
ruin of many a right excellent man.' While
taking exception to some of the moralist's sentiments, there can be no question that the policy

he inculcates is full of worldly wisdom. None knows better than you how extremely detrimental it is to all one's worldly interest, in this languid and euphuistic age, to call a spade a spade and a quack a quack. You have recently told us that at one period of your career it became inexpedient to publish your works under your own name, because on some question or other, affecting the weal of the republic of letters, you spoke your mind in forcible Saxon language. Yet this knowledge,—the knowledge that plain speech is inimical to a man's financial interests—does not now deter you from saying all you wish to say, and saying it in words as plain as those of Swift himself; so that I might appropriately apply to you the lines of Burns to Charles James Fox—

> ' My much-honour'd patron, believe your poor poet,
>   Your courage much more than your prudence you
>   show it.'

And, indeed, one never thinks of your deeds without being struck with your colossal courage. You, more markedly than most, possess that ' perfect will which no terrors can shake, which is attracted by frowns, or threats, or hostile armies ; nay, needs these to awake and fan its reserved energies into a pure flame, and is never quite itself until the hazard is extreme.' We may call you impetuous and impolitic, but we dare not deny your courage. You shoot your shafts straight at the mark, and not at some substituted simulacrum, some shade or dim adumbration set up as a decoy to deceive the public. When your dander is up, as Dandie Dinmont would say, none may approach you too closely. As Mr. Lowell said of a certain countryman of yours, when you are in the storm and tumult of battle, you are like a three-decker on fire—dangerous alike to friend and foe. Yet no one is readier to own an error or make amends for a wrong. It is not given to every man to be generous as well as just. I believe they are comparatively few who could address such lines as these to an old enemy—

> ' I would have snatched a bay-leaf from thy brow,
>   Wronging the chaplet on an honoured head ;
> In peace and charity I bring thee now
>   A lily flower instead.
>
> Pure as thy purpose, blameless as thy song,
>   Sweet as thy spirit may this offering be ;
> Forget the bitter blame that did thee wrong,
>   And take the gift from me.'

This is, I dare say, as characteristic as anything you have written, and made as great a demand on courage as any conflict in which you ever engaged.

Moreover, it is evidence that you have learned the greatest lesson which destiny has to teach—that of being true to one's-self—in other words, the necessity of overcoming all fear—fear to acknowledge a fault as well as fear to storm a stronghold. 'He has not learned the lesson of life,' says one whose silver pen you have yourself extolled, 'who does not every day surmount a fear. . . . Have the courage not to adopt another's courage. There is scope, and cause, and resistance enough for us in our proper work and circumstance. And there is no creed of an honest man, be he Christian, Turk, or Gentoo, which does not equally preach it. If you have no faith in beneficent power above you, but see only an adamantine fate coiling its folds about nature and man, then reflect that the best use of fate is to teach us courage, if only because baseness cannot change the appointed event. If you accept your thoughts as inspirations from the Supreme

Intelligence, obey them when they prescribe difficult duties, because they come only so long as they are used ; or if your scepticism reaches to the last verge, and you have no confidence in any foreign mind, then be brave, because there is one good opinion which must always be of consequence to you—namely, your own.' I do not think it will be denied by any one who has watched your career and studied your writings, that your opinions are most distinctly your own. You do not belong to the flaccid class that eternally assents ; you are not one of those who live in perpetual fear of giving offence ; nor will it be gainsaid that whatever difficult duties your conscience prescribes, you perform to the uttermost of your ability.

We may admire your courage, however, without at all concurring in your opinions. Indeed, we will admire the more because of a difference of sentiment. And for myself let me say frankly that from many of your judgments I entirely dissent. Your opinion of Goethe, for example, seems to me altogether unworthy of your perspicacity as a critic, and your liberality as a thinker. Your estimates of

George Eliot and Matthew Arnold, too, seem to me curiously unjust. When you call George Eliot a 'pragmatic rectangular prosaist,' and speak of the 'preposterous' career of the author of *Faust*, and aver that he really never lived, one is inclined to think that, like David when he slandered all mankind, you spoke in very inconsiderate haste. I for one see nothing preposterous in the career of Goethe, and I think that George Eliot, far from being a prosaist, is, except in occasional lapses, a truly creative artist. But you seem to me most unjust in denying the title of poet to Matthew Arnold. I believe with Mr. Hall Caine that there is poetry in the 'Strayed Reveller' and 'Dover Beach,' and I find 'The Youth of Nature' touching and true. The lines—

> 'Race after race, man after man,
>   Have thought that my secret was theirs,
>   Have dreamed that I lived but for them,
>   That they were my glory and joy.
>   They are dust, they are changed, they are gone !
>   I remain,'

seem to me to give out the right tone. But I am more concerned with you as an artist than as a critic.

You have been a busy worker in the realm of imagination, and, to my mind, a successful worker. You have written too much to be always at your best, but your worst is never bad. You have not had, or you have not taken, the leisure to excise, polish, and amend your productions, as among present-day poets Lord Tennyson and Mr. Lowell have done, or among past poets Pope and Gray. But you are always a poet, and invariably an artist. Many of your poems are exquisite in form, and nearly all of them attest beyond a peradventure that even at the close of the nineteenth century the spirit of poetry is still in our midst. No one can read *Balder the Beautiful*, or *The Book of Orm*, or *The City of Dream*, without being convinced (if he have an eye and ear for such things) that he is reading the work of a true poet. Nor is your prose less true or less important than your poetry.

As a novelist you work with a purpose. You descend, as you say yourself, to the heresy of instruction. Many eminent critics do hold it a heresy to descend to instruction in works of fiction, and many great authors are with the critics.   Goethe (whom you will permit me to call great), for instance, says in reference to his own *Werther*, in that autobiography which every student of literature should read, 'It cannot be expected that the public should receive an intellectual work intellectually.   In fact, it was only the subject, the material part, that was considered, as I had already found to be the case among my own friends, while at the same time arose that old prejudice, associated with the dignity of a printed book—that it ought to have a moral aim.   But a true picture of life has none.   It neither approves nor censures, but develops sentiments and actions in their consequences, and thereby enlightens and instructs.'   These are Goethe's sentiments on the subject.   He did not believe in the novel with a purpose ; nor did Scott consider himself under any necessity to be didactic.   Shakespeare, likewise, was careless of his opportunities to play the *rôle* of schoolmaster, and it is my candid opinion that Homer never really concerned himself about the moral and social welfare of his auditors.

However, the English people, though paying

little heed, as a rule, to moral instruction, like nothing better as an amusement ; and there is no valid reason for not gratifying their tastes. Moreover, it pays to have a purpose when the purpose is not flaunted too officiously in the reader's face. Dickens, in various sweet preparations, gave his readers heavy doses of ' doctrines of reform,' and they clapped their hands and shouted for joy. Mr. Besant, too, has followed in the footsteps of the author of *David Copperfield*, with very gratifying success, and Mrs. Ward has enjoyed quite a ' boom ' as a teacher and reformer. You have, therefore, precedent and example enough in writing romance with a purpose. And let it be granted without demur that in your case the process of indoctrination has been accomplished with a skill and an eloquence that give your novels a high place in the best class of didactic fiction. *The Shadow of the Sword* is, perhaps, the most powerful polemic against public war that has ever been written ; more powerful than all the orations of all the orators from Demosthenes to John Bright. Nor is it less admirable as a work of art than as a protest against the most heinous, because the most cruel and least excusable, crime that darkens the annals of mankind. The characters and situations alike are strong and telling, and abide in one's memory. In another way your *Martyrdom of Madeline* is almost as good. But I think it is in *God and the Man* that you touch high-water mark. That is a powerful, a terrible, a fascinating book. You call it 'a study of the vanity and folly of individual Hate,' and surely never before in romance was the folly of individual hate more eloquently and fearfully made manifest. Never before did human being pursue an enemy more fiercely and relentlessly than Christian Christianson, or find revenge so bitter. The character of Christian is titanic—titanic in its ferocity, its tenacity, and its ultimate nobleness. Nothing could be more savage than his appetite for vengeance, nothing more disappointing than the dead-sea fruit to which that vengeance turns in the moment of expected triumph, nothing more touching than the final sorrow and humility of the stricken soul. Like a demon he prays and blasphemes at the beginning—

' Yield up to me
This man alone of all men that I see !
Give him to me and to misery !
Give me this man if a God thou be.

But the cruel heavens all open lie,
No God doth reign o'er the sea and sky,
The earth is dark and the clouds go by,
But there is no God to hear me cry.

There is no God, none, to abolish one
Of the foul things thought, and dreamed, and done !
Wherefore I hate, till my race is run,
All living men beneath the sun.

   .   .   .   .   .   .

O Lord my God, if a God there be,
Give up the man I hate to me !
On his living heart let my vengeance feed,
And I shall know Thou art God indeed.

   .   .   .   .   .   .

The night is still, the waters sleep, the skies
Gaze down with bright innumerable eyes ;
A voice comes out of heaven and o'er the sea :
" I am ; and I will give this man to thee." '

And with the bloodthirstiness of a sleuth-
hound he tracks his prey from point to point,
on land, on sea, in green England, and amid
the snows and ice of the Polar regions, till at
last he has him fast ; and then—then vengeance swift and terrible—ah ! no, only a temporary madness, a momentary exultation, a

spasm of cruel delight in the misfortunes of Richard Orchardson, and then God smites the heart of the would-be murderer, till it melts and gushes like the hard rock in Horeb. His behaviour, when Richard Orchardson lies dying before him, is piety itself. ‘When I knew that he was dead indeed, I bent over him reverently, placed his arms down by his side, and seeing his eyes wide open, drew down the waxen lids over the sightless orbs. Then I held a little water in the palm of my hand, and cleansed the dead face ; afterwards with careful fingers arranging his hair and beard. Lastly I took one of my rude lights and set it at the corpse's head, like the death-lights we burn round dead folks in the Fens. . . . When I had ordered all in Christian cleanliness and reverence, I sat and gazed upon mine enemy. . . . Then one still morn, when the air was bright for the place and time of year, I lifted him in my arms and carried him slowly forth across the snow. I had the rude grave all ready, and now I laid him down within it, with his white face to the sky. As I stood above him, and took my last look of him, more snow began to fall. . . .

Then standing bareheaded, eager still to keep my pledge to him, I repeated, as far as I could remember, the words of the old sweet Burial Service out of our English Book of Prayer ; and when I could remember no more, I stretched out my arms in blessing, commending my enemy's soul to God. Before I had ended, his face had faded away in the falling whiteness ; and seeing it vanish utterly, I sobbed like a little child.' And so Christian Christianson has his revenge, pouring out his heart in sorrow.

The other characters are almost equally well drawn, and there are throughout the book many delightful bits of description, and situations that thrill one to the marrow ; but over these I may not now linger. Sufficient to say that so long as we have writers writing books like *God and the Man*, there is still hope for the literature of our country.

To Mr. R. D. Blackmore.

Sir,—Not many authors are regarded as classics in their own lifetime, and have their works read and treated with the admiration and reverential affection which are thought to be the meed of the great dead alone. The public seem to have an idea that Spartan treatment is best for existing writers, that their growth will be sturdier and healthier on short rations and some buffeting than on much pudding and great praise. It is all very well to honour the dead with monuments and eulogistic epitaphs, but the living should not be spoiled by being led to think too much of themselves. To be sure there are instances to prove that the public sometimes exercise a spirit of indulgence towards living authors. Sir Walter Scott had a foretaste of the honours of immortality, while he was yet the 'Shirra,' notwithstanding the chivalrous cry, as Mr. Lang calls it, of 'Burke

Sir Walter,' which, ringing and echoing in the dying man's ears, really affrighted and embittered his last moments. Coleridge and Carlyle, likewise, while still in the flesh, were allowed to possess something of the power and potency of them 'who rule our spirits from their urns,' and our Poet Laureate, while happily still enriching our literature, has more of the homage and veneration of men than most writers who have gone to that bourne whence there is no return.

But all these cases are exceptional. Posthumous honours are seldom tendered to living authors; seldomer to novelists than to any; for the common novel being hardly less ephemeral than the common newspaper, the presumption is all against the fitness of a writer of fiction for even a lower seat in the Valhalla of the gods. But it will hardly be deemed invidious, as it will certainly be no flattery, to say that the author of *Lorna Doone* is as sure of his niche in the great Temple, as any writer on the long and honourable roll of British fiction. You still write, the critics still concern themselves with your productions, but to readers at large you have passed beyond the narrow confines of criticism, and taken your place in the hearts of the people. I am not quite certain that harsh criticism of your writings would be tolerated. The Englishman is a dangerous animal when one attempts to interfere with one of his favourites, far less with one of his idols.

And, indeed, if he is content to call you great, there is no reason in the world why we should quarrel with him. It is always unsatisfactory to talk of greatness, since there is no exact standard to guide the judgment. The taste of one is not the taste of another, and to speak ill of what pleases us, or to call that great which we do not like, would be simply to be guilty of atrocious falsehood. Intrinsic merit or demerit is not susceptible of mathematical demonstration. If a reader like a book, it is totally impossible to prove that he shouldn't like it ; if he doesn't like it, all one's skill in logic and ingenuity in argument will not convince him that that book is good for him. Therefore it is idle, and worse than idle, to discuss or quarrel over some epithet, which to ninety-nine out of every hundred readers has no meaning nor intelligibility. Your best work may be greater, or may be less than the best work of our best novelists living and dead, but this much, I think, might be said with the fullest assurance, that it has as snug and secure a corner in the hearts of the people as the work of any writer of fiction, hardly excepting the Wizard of the North himself.

While the public are so tolerant and indulgent with a popular favourite as generally to read all his works, they have a singular predilection for judging him by one, for making a particular book the touchstone by which to try all his other writings. The book by which they have chosen to judge you is *Lorna Doone.* But, though that is by far your most popular book, I, for one, am not quite prepared to say it is your best. At any rate, it cannot make me forget that you are the author of *Springhaven* and *Christowell.* However, since it is the popular choice, I am quite willing to accept it as mine also, and to make it the ground on which briefly to examine the claim your admirers advance for you, of being the first of living English novelists. Without any tedious 'prelimbinaries,' as honest farmer Snowe would say, let it be frankly owned, then, that in your case the public have shown themselves marvellously good critics. They are apt to make mistakes,—indeed, if I may be permitted to use the expression, their forte seems to lie in making mistakes, but in singling out such a book as *Lorna Doone* for their warmest approval, they have shown a quite surprising acumen and accuracy of judgment. He would be a bad reader who could not enjoy that book; perhaps he would be a worse critic who would condemn him for enjoying it.

What, one is often tempted to ask, is the singular charm that fascinates us in that Romance of Exmoor? Is it in the style, or in the characters, or in the scenery and action of the story? Doubtless it lies in all these, for it is subtle and manifold. But if one were forced to lay one's finger on a particular feature as the chief one, I think it would be concluded that that gentle and humane giant, John Ridd: gentle and humane, yet full of a volcanic fire and force, and capable on occasion of being stern enough to deal out terrific justice—I say there are obvious reasons why he should be considered the central attraction of the book. And, as a matter of fact, I believe he is. A friend of mine, and one of the most discriminating of your admirers, recently spoke of the book, as a whole, and John Ridd in particular, as follows, and in so doing voiced the popular verdict: '*Lorna Doone* is one of those books which are national in character. The atmosphere is the free air of our English moors. The situations are always interesting, such common occupations as sheep-shearing and working in the fields never being prosaic. The apotheosis of brute force is natural, or it would be mean. It might still be mean if it were not allied with perfect courage and undeniable honesty and chastity. John Ridd is the type of our perfect English manhood; he has within him the element of all that is noble; nothing but manliness could dwell in his great heart. Martyrdom he would bear, but freedom he must have. He would fight like a fiend for freedom, but he would not be a libertine. It is of the John Ridds of the world that you cannot ask, "Is he a gentleman?" Such a character as Mr. Blackmore's hero stands above all questions of the kind.   He is a man. . . . Neither can criticism touch Lorna Doone herself.   She is the proper partner of John, and when that is said you have given her her due.'

It might be said that she is a very perfect heroine indeed whom criticism cannot touch— more perfect than even that sweetest and most perfect piece of fictitious womanhood, the mas- terpiece of the master, the beautiful, the peerless, the almost faultless Imogen.   However, let it be granted that Lorna Doone is the fit com- panion for the doughty yeoman of Devon. Though for myself, if I were disposed to be captious, it is on Lorna I should fasten.   It was long ago observed by a wise man that a critic, before attempting to criticise, should first of all qualify himself for his office by looking at the characters of his author from their creator's point of view, for that without that there could be no true sympathy, and without sympathy there could be no valuable criticism.   It may be that I have failed to fully grasp your intentions, or fully comprehend some of the very peculiar circumstances of the story, some of the circumstances in which Lorna is particularly involved, but to me she is not the most satisfactory female character you have drawn. Nay, I hardly think her the most satisfactory female character in the book to which she gives her name. Though palpitating with life to the finger-tips (and that, of course, is the first essential) she is not in *all* respects so fine in my eyes as either Annie or Mrs. Ridd. There are times when I think even Ruth Huckaback better. Perhaps, indeed, no character so slightly sketched as Ruth was ever truer or more intensely alive. She has a woman's heart in that little body of hers, a heart that swells with big passions, and such aspirations as only a woman can have, and, little as we see of her, we know her thoroughly, and what is more, sympathise with her deeply.

Lorna Doone we also know thoroughly, and in most of her trying situations sympathise with. But she hardly commands complete and perfect sympathy and admiration. How is it that a creation, in most respects so charming, fails to make the reader, as it were, her own, through at least the first half of the book ? Is it because, like Juliet, she is sometimes too much the untutored child of nature to suit the modern taste, or is it because the over-generous John, seeing her with the eyes of infatuation, makes her just a little too angelic, and thus sometimes lifts her beyond the sphere of our sympathy? Perhaps the latter is the true explanation. It would be interesting to find that once in a while, however long the intervals might be, John was aware of some slight human imperfection in his adored inamorata. It is so human to be fallible, that when we encounter a creature of divine perfection, much as we admire her, we can hardly feel that bond of equality and kinship which alone makes one child of Adam interesting to another. Perhaps the fact that John Ridd is unable to discover, or at any rate declines to reveal any trifling defect in Lorna, is a strong argument against the autobiographical form of fiction. John is always ready enough to dwell, and dwell with emphasis, on his own imperfections, but it evidently is a sheer impossibility to see any fault, hardly so much as a foible in the goddess of the Doone Glen. Perhaps it would be too much to expect the stern fidelity in a

lover on which Cromwell insisted in the painter
of his portrait. Nature may deal in warts and
wrinkles, but lovers obviously do not. To point
out the blemishes in one's mistress were, perhaps, to declare one's-self a monster. Hence
it might be considered unfortunate when it falls
to the lot of a lover, so fervent and single as
John Ridd, to paint the picture of the heroine
of such a book as *Lorna Doone.* The painter
is so zealous a worshipper of his subject that
he forgets the shadows ; and I believe it is an
axiom of art that the shades are no less essential
to the perfect portrait than the lights. After all
the objections that might justly be taken to what
is styled the analytical school, a little more of
its spirit would have saved the delineator of
Lorna Doone from giving us an angel instead
of a woman. But let it be frankly owned that,
even with her fault of a too elaborate perfection,
Lorna Doone is a splendid creation, noble in
all her instincts, and hardly suffering in a comparison with any heroine of any novelist living
or dead, except, perhaps, some of the heroines
of Goethe, and one or two of Mr. Howells's.

Concerning the hero, the titanic John, there

can, I think, be but one opinion, the opinion given by the critic I have already quoted, namely, that he ' is the type of our perfect English manhood.' A grand, massive character he surely is, the embodiment of English strength, English solidity, English generosity, English fair-play—a right sound piece of stuff, true as the best-tempered steel, not to be shaken by adversity, nor spoiled by prosperity—a yeoman of whom one would be proud to say that his limbs were made in England. It is hard to speak of John Ridd without going into super-latives. He is so frank, so genial, of such vast dimensions in mind and body, so caressing in his gentleness, so terrific in his anger, so just, so honourable, so fierce in his hatred of all that is mean, so constant in his loyalty to all that is noble, so perfectly admirable in his strength and his weakness, that it is admiration first and criti-cism nowhere. Some of Scott's characters would, I dare say, equal him in strength and kindli-ness of nature. He somewhat resembles Dandie Dinmont. Not that there is the least trace of imitation in him, but that great natures are pretty much the same the wide world over, and that when they are faithfully drawn there must be points of similarity in the pictures. Others of Scott's characters, too, might match him in most of his best qualities—many of them are much more romantic,—but since the days of Scott I doubt if any novelist has given us a character fit to stand beside John Ridd, except it might be the creators of Christian Christianson and Daniel Mylrea.

For one of his physical proportions John Ridd is gentle almost beyond example. As the saying is, he would not hurt a fly if he could help it, and his behaviour towards Lorna and his mother and sisters is very beautiful. At the same time, though gentleness is admirable in a giant, I don't know that I like Ridd's softness best. Dr. Johnson professed to like a good hater, and I own that I am partial to a man who knows how to be angry on occasion. A man's mettle is shown by the manner in which he deals with an enemy; and perhaps no incident in Ridd's career is more impressive than that final meeting with Carver Doone, after the chivalrous outlaw had shot Lorna at the altar. It was a situation to try a man; but

John rises magnificently to the occasion.   Not long after the outlaw has taken his base revenge, John is able to announce that 'the black bog had him by. the feet, the sucking of the ground drew on him like the thirsty lips of death.   In our fury we had heeded neither wet nor dry ; nor thought of earth beneath us.   I myself might scarcely leap with the last spring of o'erlaboured legs from the engulfing grave of slime.   He fell back with his swarthy breast (from which my grip had rent all the clothing) like a hummock of bog oak, standing out of the quagmire ; and then he tossed his arms to heaven, and they were black to the elbow.   I could only gaze and pant, for my strength was no more than an infant's, from the fury and the horror.   Scarcely could I turn away while joint by joint he sank from sight.'   John Ridd can be gentle, but he knows how to avenge a wrong.

Nor with all his delicious self-depreciation, his apparent heaviness and ignorance of life and literature (except the Bible and Master William Shakespeare), is he wanting in what the Scotch call 'wut.'   Like Falstaff, he hath a very pleasant humour. It rises spontaneously and unexpectedly, as the best humour always does and must, and ripples like sunshine over scenes which would otherwise be exceedingly grim indeed. His accounts of his own escapades, especially in the early portions of the book, are done with a delightful sense of the charm of lightenment. But this quality of humour is one which is ever present in all your works. You cannot even make a parson arrest a thief without indulging in a little jocoseness, just enough to give savour to the scene without destroying the excitement of it.

Besides the quality of humour, your characters are usually endowed with very considerable powers of observation and reflection. John Ridd, indeed, is a second Sancho Panza in the liberal fashion in which he lets pearls of wisdom drop by the way. 'Now, while I was walking daily in and out,' he says, during one of his visits to London, 'among great crowds of men (few of whom had any freedom from the cares of money, and many of whom were even morbid with a worse pest called politics) I could not be quit of thinking how we jostle one another.

God has made the earth quite large, with a spread of land enough for all to live on without fighting, also a mighty spread of water, laying hands on sand and cliff with a solemn voice in storm time, and in the gentle weather moving men to thoughts of equity. This as well is full of food, being two-thirds of the world, and reserve for devouring knowledge, by the time the sons of men have fed away the dry land. Yet before the land itself has acknowledged touch of man upon one in a hundred acres, and before one mile in ten thousand of the exhaustless ocean has ever felt the plunge of hook or the combing of the haul nets, lo! we crawl in flocks together upon the hot ground that stings us, even as the black grubs crowd upon the harried cattle. Surely we are given too much to follow the tracks of each other.'

That is a bit of philosophy that might well be conned even in this enlightened era.

One great charm, not only of *Lorna Doone*, but of all your works, lies in the warmth of tone that pervades them. Not only are your creations vital (in *Springhaven* they are fairly exuberant with life), but we seem to feel the pulse of Nature in your scenic pictures as well. At the start I asked whether the charm of *Lorna Doone* lay in the style. I think it might be answered that, if the chief pleasure in reading your writings is not derivable from style, at least your style gives no small pleasure to every reader with any appreciation of culture. It is a style that is peculiar and hard to analyse. Sometimes, in its expressiveness, it reminds one of the style of John Bunyan, at other times its circumstantial minuteness reminds one of Defoe's ; but, as a whole, it is infinitely richer than Bunyan's, and infinitely more poetic than Defoe's. Perhaps its power is shown nowhere as well as in the descriptions of Nature which abound in all your writings. The following, I think, gives evidence of what is called the poetic sense :—

‘ The rising of the sun was noble in the cold and warmth of it ; peeping down the spread of light, he raised his shoulder heavily over the edge of gray mountain and wavering length of upland. Beneath his gaze the dewfogs dipped, and crept to the hollow places, then stole away in line and column holding skirts, and clinging subtly at the sheltering corners where rock hung over grass-land, while the brave lines of the hills came forth, one beyond other gliding.

'Then the woods arose in folds, like drapery of awakened mountains, stately, with a depth of awe and memory of the tempests. Autumn's mellow hand was on them, as they owned already, touched with gold and red and olive; and their joy towards the sun was less to a bridegroom than a father.

'Yet before the floating impress of the woods could clear itself, suddenly the gladsome light leaped over hill and valley, casting amber, blue, and purple, and a tint of rich, red rose according to the scene they lit on, and the curtain flung around; yet all alike dispelling fear and the cloven hoof of darkness; all on the wings of hope advancing, and proclaiming, "God is here."'

Somehow I imagine that your success as a portrait-painter hinders a due appreciation of your merits as a landscape artist. It is a pity to think that such a passage as the above should be skipped.

MARK TWAIN.

To Mr. MARK TWAIN.

Sir,—I am writing to you because I think you would like to hear from me, and I am sending the letter to the public press because it is fashionable. Every man of any pretension does that now, and the more private and confidential the letter is, the more papers he sends it to; so, as I hate to lag behind the times, I am following the fashion. In past ages, you know —say about the year 1492, when your illustrious and acquisitive ancestor, John Morgan Twain, crossed the Atlantic with Columbus, and on landing deftly 'solde ye anchor to ye dam sauvages from ye interior; saying yt he hadde found it, ye sonne of a ghun'—about the time this philanthropist emigrated to America to look after the morals of the Indians by erecting a jail and a gallows, it was not thought 'good form' to have private letters publicly printed. It would then have been considered affectation to do anything of the sort. In those ridiculously fastidious times people wrote to each other under the strictest seal of secrecy, as if they were conspirators plotting a general assassination of everybody worth killing, or thieves planning a national burglary, and no one had any fun when they called each other names, or were any the wiser when they insinuated that they could tell tales an they liked. We do things better now. If this is not precisely a simple it is an ingenuous age, and has nothing to hide. All is done above board, and we don't give a continental (by the way, what 's a continental?) if the whole world, and what 's more, the world's wife, read all we write.

To be sure there are old-fashioned people hid away in nooks and corners of the earth, who follow the customs of preceding ages and still seal their letters. You hear these deluded creatures sometimes in a stationer's shop asking for well-gummed envelopes, as if they would launch us back to antediluvian epochs ; but the absurd and exclusive habit of giving a letter to the party to whom it is addressed only is dying out, like the belief in ghosts, and angels, and

miracles, and the Bible and other old superstitions. Oh, the world's getting along, never
you fear! It's a good deal smarter to-day than
it was fifty years ago. You may bet on that. As
the old woman said—I think she was a negress
of South Carolina — 'things is pergressin'.'
We don't take much stock in the exploded
ideas of our fathers and grandfathers. We
have ideas of our own, and are not beholden
to anybody,—not to Solomon, nor Socrates,
nor Carlyle, nor any of that tribe. The
youngest child among us wouldn't be taken in
by Moses, for example, after the dressing down
Colonel Ingersoll has given him. The old law-
giver made a great many mistakes in his day.
He was careless, you see, and his reputation's
ruined. And then he didn't know quite so
much as he pretended. Colonel Ingersoll
knows a heap more than ever Moses dreamed
of knowing. Science didn't flourish to any
great extent amongst the Jewish Patriarchs.
Moses never was at college, and couldn't be
expected to be 'well up.' Moreover, there
were no telegraphs, or telephones, or stock
exchanges, or city councils, or lecture platforms,

or encyclopædias, or literary men like you and me, or debating clubs, or public-houses in his day. The engines of civilisation were wanting —sadly wanting; so that it is clear at a glance Colonel Ingersoll must of necessity be a superior person to Moses. For what makes one man superior to another? Education, to be sure, and the privilege of reading such books as *A Tramp Abroad.* Books like that open up the mind and throw light on the dark recesses of the soul. They show one the immensity of human ignorance — in times past: they are great civilising agents. ' Worth makes the man, and want of it the fellow,' says Pope; but it is clear he meant education and wrote worth only to suit the exigencies of verse. This proves, you see, that verse is a cramped kind of composition, and that all men who wish to be understood will steer clear of it. A man can't get in the precise meaning he would like in verse, and it is trying to get it in that makes so many of our poets bald. A curious essay might be written on ' Wherefore are poets so bald ? ' though the answer might be succinctly given, ' Because they tear out their hair.' Between

the question and the answer, however, you
could get in a great deal of interesting matter,
and you might have a nice enjoyable little
chuckle at the expense of Mr. Besant, who
seriously advises young writers to write a sonnet
daily before dinner, for the purpose—not of
giving them an appetite—but of improving their
style.   I think your own suggestion that authors
should begin their career by eating a couple of
medium-sized whales is more sensible ; for fish
gives one brain power, while sonnets are too
often sapless and innutritious.   But I seem to
be getting away from my subject.

I was talking of the beautiful and, happily,
growing custom of having private letters printed
in books, newspapers, and public journals.   It
is a beautiful custom, for it lets the reading
public—a section of mankind I greatly reverence—see how smart a man is, and how neatly
he can turn his phrases, and how aptly he can
hit the other fellow on the head and knock
him sprawling, thus yielding both amusement
and edification ; so I am sending this as a kind
of open letter that people may judge impartially

between you and me. That's fair you see; the public are not deprived of their rights, and you are prevented from poking fun at my mistakes; for you must understand the printer undertakes to do the square thing by this letter. He says if my lucubration (he doesn't use the word disrespectfully, it's just his way of talking) is legibly written on one side of the paper only (it's economy to write on both sides, but he won't have it), and doesn't contain more than a thousand libels, nor more than two hundred grammatical mistakes, and has some odd ideas people would like to get a hold of, he'll print it under a pretty and conspicuous heading, with the name of the addressee given correctly —to the best of his ability. (I suppose the last clause is intended as a sort of satire on my penmanship, which is neither very clear nor conspicuously elegant.) The spelling and punctuation he undertakes to look after himself, and the printer's devil—no, I guess it's the printer's reader—takes care that, on an average, not more than half the letters in a word attempt to stand on their heads, and that no stray sheep, so to speak, sneak in amongst them. That's our compact; so that you may say I'm responsible for the sense and sentiments, and he's responsible for mostly everything besides. Should you, therefore, discover any egregious errors not directly connected with the sense or the sentiment, you are at liberty to publicly expose them; but should you discover anything ridiculous, either in the opinions expressed or in the style of writing, perhaps you would be good enough to communicate with me privately. That seems all that need be said on that head, and now we'll settle down to business.

I want to tell you in a plain way just what I think of you. I am impelled to do this from a sense of public duty, for I think there are mistaken notions entertained of your works. It will be my business to set the popular judgment right.

You will, no doubt, be gratified to learn that I have found your works very consoling in times of trouble and affliction. And it doesn't in the least detract from my enjoyment of them that I clearly perceive you intended them to be, not pathetic, but funny. After all, what matters it what one intended? One cannot always carry out one's intentions, and one sometimes mistakes one's forte. Some people start with the idea that they are great poets, others that they are great novelists, others that they are great artists, others that they are great humorists, others that they are great sages and philosophers, others that they are great generals, and so forth; and very often they carry their delusions with them to the grave. Delusions can do no harm there; still it is always better to leave them in their natural place in the great inane above. But while this is so, one shouldn't be too hard on people for their mistakes; and far be it from me to say a word in censure of you for imagining that your forte lies in raising a laugh, while all the time it lies in drawing tears.

You are excruciatingly pathetic. Sterne, mourning over an ass, and refusing to be comforted, is positively hilarious compared with you in your account of *My late Senatorial Secretaryship*, or *The Facts in the Case of the Great Beef Contract*, or *Journalism in Tennessee*, or *Niagara*. That description of the Indian attack on you is very touching. 'It was the greatest operation that ever was. I simply saw a sudden flash in the air of clubs, brickbats, fists, bead-baskets, and mocassins—a single flash, and they all appeared to hit me at once, and no two of them in the same place. In the next instant the entire tribe was upon me. They tore half the clothes off me, they broke my arms and legs, they gave me a thump that dented the top of my head till it would hold coffee like a saucer; and to crown their disgraceful proceedings, and add insult to injury, they threw me over the Niagara Falls, and I got wet.' Nor is that the most touching part of it; for after you had gone round and round forty-four times in the eddy at the foot of the falls, ‘a man walked down, and sat down, and put a pipe in his mouth, and lit a match, and followed me with one eye, and kept the other on the match, while he sheltered it in his hands from the wind,’ without offering to render you any assistance whatever. ‘Presently a ·puff of wind blew it (the match) out. The next time I swept round, he said—

‘ “ Got a match ? ”

‘ “ Yes, in my other vest. Help me out, please.”

' " Not for Joe."

' When I came round again, I said : " Excuse the seemingly impertinent curiosity of a drowning man, but will you explain this singular conduct of yours ? "

' " With pleasure. I am the coroner. Don't hurry on my account. I can wait for you. But I wish I had a match."

' I said : " Take my place, and I 'll go and get you one."

' He declined. This lack of confidence on his part created a coldness between us, and from that time forward I avoided him. It was my idea, in case anything happened to me, to so time the occurrence as to throw my custom into the hands of the opposition coroner over on the American side.

' At last a policeman came along, and arrested me for disturbing the peace by yelling at the people on shore for help. The judge fined me, but I had the advantage of him. My money was in my pantaloons, and my pantaloons were with the Indians.

' Thus I escaped. I am now lying in a very critical condition. At least I am lying, anyway,

critical or not critical. I am hurt all over ; but
I cannot tell the full extent yet, because the
doctor is not done taking the inventory. He
will make out my manifest this evening. However, thus far he thinks that only sixteen of my
wounds are fatal.'

Was there ever a more touching tale of
cruelty more wanton, or more heroically borne.
The injustice is colossal. Not only were you
hurt all over, not only did you sustain sixteen
fatal wounds—perhaps more, but sixteen for a
certainty—but you got wet, probably indeed
drenched, and thus ran a serious risk of getting
your joints askew with rheumatism. The Indians were brutes, the coroner was a brute, the
policeman was a brute, the judge was a brute.
There is no evidence that you exaggerate ; your
story has every appearance of truth ; and being
true and simply told, without literary flourishes,
or any attempt to draw on the reservoirs of the
reader, it is all the more affecting. My eyes
are suffused with tears as I write. I feel my
heart swelling and welling with soft dewy pity
(that's a pet phrase from the poets), and I am
drawn towards you in the bonds of brotherhood.

You are a human creature like myself, alas ! you are too, too human, and your mountain of troubles is too, too solid, and refuses to melt ; and the canon of destiny is aimed straight at you (kindly compare with the speech of Hamlet, the rollicking Prince of Denmark). You know what it is to be in tribulation ; you know what it is not only to suffer in the body, but in the soul—in the soul, sir. Ay, that is where the rub is most poignantly felt. Nobody can see into the soul ; it is a great vacuum, an invisible something or other that folks are not very sure of, but it hurts awfully sometimes. In speaking of it you cannot say, with any semblance of truth, that the sting goes to the quick, for there is no quick ; nor the dagger to the marrow, for there is no marrow ; but, ugh ! doesn't a wound in it make you cry out ?

You know the acute suffering of the soul, and it is because of this that I always recommend your books to people in sorrow in preference to books that are avowedly devotional. I specially recommend them to such as have suffered bereavement—such as have lost darling pugs, or dear little tame rats, or gentle pet cats that have, perhaps, been horribly mutilated by vicious steel traps when walking abroad to pay social visits in the cool of the evening. I have seen these bereaved and inconsolable ones palpably falling into a decline; I have known their friends to get estimates from undertakers in sad anticipation of what was coming; I have known the poor unfortunates to take leave of their families and fold their hands and await the inevitable; and I have gone and put one of your works into their hands, and lo! as if by magic, they began to mend. You can never know the number of the people you have snatched from death and the grave. You are the greatest physician alive. Your medicines work cures that are perfectly miraculous. O sir, the world owes you a debt of gratitude it can never, never, never repay!

Let us say that some estimable lady has lost a pet pug that has been the solace of her life for ever so many years. The poor little affectionate, docile thing has, perhaps, died from want of breath, the windpipe having closed from a surplus of fat—an awful death, a most affecting death even to think of. Naturally the estimable lady is stricken beyond expression. Her grief is too great for tears. The heart has been blasted. The seat of the affections has been rocked like a ship in a hurricane. It may be that the throne of reason itself has been invaded. What are you to expect in such a case? It seems hopeless. The hand of death is on the estimable owner of the late lamented pug. She is doomed. She must go. That is the natural supposition. But some one puts one of your touching and tender books into her hands. At first she reads languidly and without interest, feeling that she has done with this world; but by-and-by, and almost unconsciously, she begins to turn the pages with some show of enjoyment, then her feelings are touched, then a nice cooling little stream begins to course down either cheek, and the hot eyes have a refreshing bath, and the heavy heart is relieved of its pent-up—what the deuce is pent-up in the heart? Never mind, the pent-up heart is relieved, and the estimable lady, feeling that she is not alone in her sorrow, that you have suffered before her, picks herself up, puts on her best bonnet and her sweetest smile, and goes to look up a successor to her dear departed. And that is why I recommend your books.

But a curious thing happened to me lately. A friend of mine was going to a funeral, and, having to travel a considerable distance by rail, he thought unto himself that he would like something to read. Now he imagined it would be rather disrespectful to the departed to take up a secular newspaper, so he consulted me.

'I can give you what you want exactly,' I said, and with cheerful confidence put *The New Pilgrim's Progress* into his hand. 'I know that will suit you,' I said, as he stepped into the train. 'If you're not as sober and solemn as a judge pronouncing a death sentence when you reach your destination, you may call me a Dutchman.' Now the funny thing is he never has called me a Dutchman, but two days later I received the book back by post, with a note of three lines couched in very formal style, intimating that he had a natural dislike to being made the butt of a clumsy and blasphemous jest. I demanded what he meant, and this is what he said, 'Do you call that gigantic and persistent humbug religious? Why, the man is perfectly incapable of writing the truth. **He can't describe a** single thing as he saw it, or as **it really is. He says he acted as** second to Gambetta in a duel with **some fool or other,** and actually proposed brickbats at three-quarters of a mile. The thing is ridiculous; it's **monstrous; it**'s simply a lie,—that's what it is. **Again, he says that once during a** thunderstorm, **by actual count, the** lightning struck at his **establishment—his** establishment, **indeed!—** seven hundred and sixty-four times in forty **minutes, and** tripped on a rod and slipped down some spiral twist and shot into the earth before it had time to be surprised at the way the thing was done. **Isn't that a likely story?** And again, when **he is in Rome (where they should have kept him) he gives it out as a sober fact that he discovered a theatrical** programme nearly **two thousand** years old among the ruins of the Coliseum, and that this bit of paper was as fresh as the day it was printed. To make the lie complete he should have **said it was** fresher. **And then when he is in the** Holy Land—mind **you,** in the Holy Land—his silly blasphemies

might be pardoned elsewhere on the score of
weakness of intellect, but in the Holy Land they
are unforgivable,—well, what do you think this
fine writer of yours asserts as a solemn fact? He
asserts that outside a certain mosque is a minia-
ture temple, which marks the spot where David
and Goliath used to sit and judge the people.
Did ever sane man, professing to be a Christian,
and having some knowledge of his Bible, print
such a statement as that before. Such colossal
ignorance astounded me. Nor is that all, nor
half, nor quarter, nor the tenth part, nor the
hundredth, nor the millionth of his absurdities.
He tells us, for instance, about a horse he
owned by the name of 'Jericho,' and calmly
remarks it was a mare. Well, this mare or
horse, or mule or ass, or whatever it was, had a
practice of fighting the flies with its heels,
because it had no tail, and it used also to
reach round and bite the rider's legs. He
says he didn't care for that, only he didn't like
to see a horse too sociable. I ask you, is that
likely? I ask you, is it sensible? But why go
on citing instances of the man's monstrosity?
He is utterly unreliable; he is a fraud; you

don't know when he is attempting to palm off some gigantic falsehood as a fact. And yet this is the writer you would recommend to one in distress; this is the writer you would put into my hand when I was going away to a dear friend's funeral. Get out of my house, sir; let me never see your face again—go out of this, and go to —— with your Mark Twain.' That is how the interview closed. I tried to reason with him. I tried to show him that you sometimes attempted a little jest, and that when a man intends a thing as a joke he should not be harshly criticised for unveracity, even when the joke is not so obvious as to make one laugh. But he declined to listen to me, and as I noticed a curious restlessness about the toe of his right boot, I departed. We have not spoken since.

But his was an exceptional case, and in general I find, as already stated, that your works are very soothing. With old ladies and gentlemen, with no perception of humour and no liking for it, they are particularly successful. An old maiden lady who had just buried her thirty-seventh cat recently said to me, 'Heaven bless Mr. Twain; he made me cry for two hours,—two long hours; it was so delicious. He's not frivolous, you know, like some you read; he never attempts to make you laugh —oh, he's so nice and feeling!'

THE END.

Printed by T. and A. Constable, Printers to Her Majesty, *at the Edinburgh University Press.*